First-Rate Reading™ ^Basics

Vocabulary Grades 1-2

by Starin W. Lewis

Carson-Dellosa Publishing Company, Inc. • Greensboro, North Carolina

Credits and Dedication

Project Director:

Kelly Gunzenhauser

Editor:

Erin Seltzer Hensley

Layout Design:

Jon Nawrocik

Inside Illustrations:

Stefano Giorgi

Cover Design:

Peggy Jackson

Cover Illustrations:

Stefano Giorgi

This book is dedicated to my former students. Thank you for the many years of laughter, learning, and inspiration.

-S. L.

ISBN 1-59441-050-X

Table of Contents

Introduction

Understanding vocabulary is an essential part of reading. If students do not understand the words they are reading, they will not understand the text as a whole. Lack of vocabulary skills can cause a vicious cycle. Students who struggle excessively with new words usually do not want to read. Without reading, students are less likely to learn new words. Break the cycle by teaching students vocabulary skills.

Research shows that people learn vocabulary in two ways—indirectly and directly. Students learn most vocabulary indirectly through having conversations with each other and adults, and through listening to stories. Another indirect way students learn vocabulary is through extensive independent reading. There is an indirect instruction mini-unit at the beginning of this book; however, since most indirect instruction is embedded in students' daily lives, the majority of this book focuses on direct instruction.

Direct vocabulary instruction helps students learn words and skills that they may not understand through indirect instruction alone. There are two main types of direct instruction. One type introduces new vocabulary words before reading. The other type teaches students how to use word-learning strategies to figure out new vocabulary words. The specific word instruction section of this book provides pre-reading activities and extended instruction. Students will learn to use reference aids, such as dictionaries and glossaries; analyze word parts; and learn how to use context clues to decipher the meanings of words.

Utilize the Parent Letter reproducible (page 4) to help reinforce vocabulary instruction at home. The Parent Letter helps inform parents about which skills they impart to their children while talking to them and reading aloud, and also offers suggestions for how to build prior knowledge.

Finally, use the Assessment (page 5) to review students' vocabulary skills at any time during the school year, including before instruction begins. Assessing early will help you determine in which areas students need practice. It will also help you group students by skill level, even if your preference is to group students with a range of skills.

Name _____

Parent Letter

Dear Parents/Family:

Research shows that good readers are more successful in school. Reading is used in all other subjects and is critical for success in real life. It is important for your child to develop a solid reading base that extends beyond phonics into other areas such as vocabulary. Following are suggestions and information about this area of instruction.

Readers need good **vocabularies** because they must know most of the words in the text to comprehend it. Children must have good oral vocabularies (words they speak and hear) as well as written vocabularies (words they write and read). Help your child improve vocabulary skills by doing the following:

- Expose your child to many oral language experiences. Children learn a great part of their vocabulary indirectly—by being exposed to new vocabulary. Let your child engage in conversation with you and other adults, and do not use "baby talk" or "watered down" vocabulary.
- Read aloud to your child often. Include books that are above your child's reading level. Students' listening comprehension levels are higher than their reading levels, so they usually understand text that is being read to them. Pause when you come to new words to define and discuss them. Tell your child to stop you if you read words that are not familiar.
- Encourage your child to read independently as often as possible. Surround your child with literature.
- Finally, students indirectly learn vocabulary through new experiences. These experiences build what is referred to as "prior knowledge." Prior knowledge plays a major role in students' comprehension and vocabulary acquisition. Experiences can be simple or elaborate.

Using these ideas will help your child begin to enjoy reading. For more information, please feel free to contact me.

Sincerely,

_____

First-Rate Reading™: Vocabulary • CD-104020 • © Carson-Dellosa
Basics

Name _____

Date _____

Assessment

Score: ___ /10

Write the following words on index cards: *cat, moon, sun, math,* and *mug.* Use these cards with questions 1–3.

1. Place the words *sun, cat,* and *moon* in front of the student. Ask the student to place the words in alphabetical order. (*cat, moon, sun*)

2. Place the words *mug, moon,* and *math* in front of the student. Ask the student to place the words in alphabetical order. (*math, moon, mug*)

3. Place the words *math* and *sun* at the top of the desk. Tell the student that these two words are guide words in a dictionary. Ask, "Which of the remaining words would be on this dictionary page?" (*moon, mug*)

4. Ask, "What is a glossary?" (A dictionary that contains only words found in a particular book or other text. Answers will vary.)

5. Write the contraction *she'll* on an index card. Show the student the card. Ask, "What two words make this contraction?" (*she, will*)

6. Write the words *do not* on an index card. Show the student the card. Ask, "What contraction could you make?" (*don't*)

7. Write the word *sunset* on an index card. Ask, "Is this a compound word? Why?" (Yes. It is made from the two smaller words *sun* and *set.*)

8. Ask, "What does the prefix *un-* mean?" (It means *not, the opposite of,* or *to remove.* Answers will vary.)

9. Ask, "What does *s* at the end of a word like *cars* mean?" (It means there is more than one car. The letter *s* makes the word plural.)

10. Read the sentence "The black exhaust from the bus made the girl cough." Ask the student, "What do you think the word *exhaust* means?" (Gas, smoke, or fumes that are produced by an engine. Answers will vary.)

Indirect Instruction

Daily Oral Language: Introduction

Research has shown that when children have conversations with people, especially adults, they indirectly learn vocabulary words. In these conversations, children may hear words repeated several times. They also hear unfamiliar words. The more conversations children have, the better their vocabulary skills will be.

Conversation Party

Have a conversation party with students. Explain that the point of the party is for students to have conversations with adults. Tell students that when they have conversations with adults, they will learn more words. Work with students to write invitations with RSVPs. On the invitations, explain the purpose of the party: students learn vocabulary indirectly from other people. Saying words in conversation gives students repeated exposure to vocabulary. Also, adults use words that may be new to students, and students learn these words from conversations. Allow each student to invite one adult to school. Ask staff members, such as the principal, the librarian, a special education teacher, etc., to attend the party to ensure that there are enough adults. On the day of the party, pair each student with an adult partner. Write the following conversation starters on the board:

I always laugh when . . .
My favorite part of first (or second) grade is (or was) . . .
The best book I ever read was _____ because . . .
For fun, I like to . . .
The best trip I ever had was . . .

Let each pair choose one sentence starter to begin a conversation. Remind the whole group that the sentence starters may spark other conversations. These other subjects are acceptable; the objective is to get children and adults talking. At the end of the party, thank everyone for coming and encourage the adults and students to continue talking to each other in the future.

Casual Interview

Encourage students to have conversations with their family members by setting up opportunities for family interviews. Explain that an interview is a meeting in which information is gained from someone. Give each student a copy of the Casual Interview reproducible (page 7). Have each student take home a reproducible, ask a family member the questions, write the responses, and bring the sheet back to school. (Family members may help younger students with bigger words on the reproducible.) The next day, ask, "What did you learn about your family members that you didn't know? Did you hear any new words? Which questions were your favorites?" Continue your conversation with students by asking more questions about the interviews.

Name _____   *Indirect Instruction*

Casual Interview

Dear Parents/Family,

Did you know that talking with children helps them develop vocabulary skills? It does! Please listen to your child read these questions and share your answers with your child. Feel free to start conversations about the questions.

1. What is your favorite animal? Why?

_____

_____

2. Who is your best friend? What do you like about him or her?

_____

_____

3. When you were in school, what was your favorite subject? Why?

_____

_____

4. What is your favorite book? Why?

_____

_____

5. What is your favorite movie? Why?

_____

_____

First-Rate Reading™: Vocabulary • CD-104020 • © Carson-Dellosa
Basics

7

Listening to Adults Read: Introduction

When students listen to adults read, they indirectly learn new vocabulary. Students not only hear a model for fluent reading, but are also exposed to rich and interesting vocabulary. "Thinking aloud" when reading unfamiliar words teaches students reading strategies. In addition, talking about books encourages conversation—another indirect method for teaching vocabulary.

Book Awards

Give students another reason to listen to books by creating class book awards. Make one copy of the Book Awards reproducible (page 9). Write four nominations for best books in each category. When the nominations are complete, make a class set of the reproducible. Explain what the categories Best Illustrations, Best Comedy, Best Drama, and Best Mystery mean. Each week, check out library books from one category. The category for the first week is Best Illustrations. Each day for four days, read one nominee from that category to the class and have students write its title on the reproducible. On the fifth day, have each student vote for the book with the best illustrations by circling the number beside the title of that book on a Book Awards reproducible. After circling her favorite, have her cut out that category and place her ballot in a box. (If desired, allow students to decorate a box to look like a ballot box.) Continue in the same manner with the remaining categories. After the voting is complete, have an awards ceremony. Ask four students to design an award for each category and reveal the winners to the class. Attach the awards to color copies of the winning titles' book covers and display them on a bulletin board titled "And the Winner Is . . ."

Guest Readers

Having other readers visit the classroom improves students' vocabulary and keeps things interesting. Students like to hear different voices and to meet school staff members with whom they may not interact very often. Invite several adults who work at the school, such as the cafeteria manager, the building manager, a custodian, a school secretary, etc., to read books to the class. If any of the adults are nervous about selecting books, offer to help them choose appropriate titles. Also consider giving a few tips about reading aloud, such as how to hold the book and show pictures, how to talk about vocabulary words, and how to interact with students. Schedule guest readers several days apart so that students will be fresh and ready when the guests read. Introduce each guest and help spark conversations after the readings, if necessary. Use conversation starters, such as, "Did you like the book?" "Have you read it before?" or "If you were the author of the book, would you change anything?"

Book Awards

Circle the number of your favorite title for each category. Cut out the ballot and place it in the ballot box.

Nominees for Best Illustrations
1. _____
2. _____
3. _____
4. _____

Nominees for Best Comedy
1. _____
2. _____
3. _____
4. _____

Nominees for Best Drama
1. _____
2. _____
3. _____
4. _____

Nominees for Best Mystery
1. _____
2. _____
3. _____
4. _____

Extensive Independent Reading: Introduction

The more children read independently, the more they are exposed to new words. The best readers often have the best vocabularies. When reading becomes more frustrating than fun, students often stop reading. Without reading independently, students are exposed to fewer words and reading new texts becomes even more difficult. Making independent reading enjoyable and feasible for students is another way to provide indirect vocabulary instruction.

My Favorite Things

Encourage students to read independently and encourage their love for reading by empowering them to choose reading materials. Motivate students to read by focusing on subjects that interest them. Give each student a copy of the My Favorite Things reproducible (page 11). Have each student list five of her favorite things. Invite students to include things like *birds, drawing, sports*—things that interest them. After students have listed their favorite things, take the class to the school library and help each student select a book about one of her five listed interests. Although students can read at higher levels if they are truly interested in given topics, make sure books are appropriately leveled for students' abilities. Tell students to write the titles of their books on their reproducibles. Allow time during the day for students to read their books. When students are finished, have them choose books for other topics from their "favorites" lists. Continue until each student has completed a book about each favorite thing she listed on her reproducible. Encourage students to choose books about other fun topics on a regular basis.

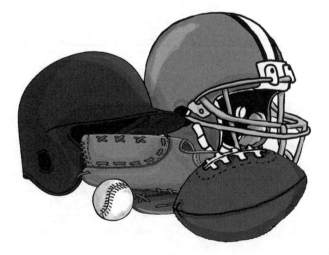

Light Reading Marathon

Motivate students to read more by making reading as fun as possible. Any kind of reading is positive. Adults often choose light reading for leisure time. The same should be true for children. Encourage students to turn to reading for fun. Pick a day for a light reading marathon and have students bring in comic books, cartoon collections, magazines, and joke books. Consider sending note homes to remind students to bring their books on the correct day and also to explain the reasoning behind the marathon. Explain to families that the usual school reading day is made up of fiction, nonfiction, and historical fiction. The light reading marathon gives students a wider variety of reading materials, motivates them to read, and provides new vocabulary. If students do not have light reading materials at home, take the class to the school library to choose appropriate materials. On the special day, allow students to read on the floor. Reserve a block of time during the day for the marathon so that students can have uninterrupted reading time. If students enjoy the light reading marathon, also use it as a reward for good class behavior.

My Favorite Things

Write five of your favorite things.

1. _____

2. _____

3. _____

4. _____

5. _____

Write the titles of books you will read about your favorite things.

1. _____

2. _____

3. _____

4. _____

5. _____

Specific Word Instruction

Pre-Reading Strategies: Introduction

When students do not understand vocabulary words in text, their comprehension is affected. One strategy to help students with difficult words is to preview text. This section provides numerous strategies for understanding unfamiliar words prior to reading. Remind students that learning new words before reading helps them understand specific words, and in turn, the meaning of the text.

Book Bounce

Ahead of time, look through a text that will be in a current reading lesson. Find three or four words that will be important to comprehending the text. Make notes about the selected words and their page numbers. At the beginning of the lesson, explain that "Book Bounce" is a phrase that means previewing text before reading it. Instead of looking at every word on every page, tell students they will "bounce" around the book. Direct students to the first selected word in the book and read the surrounding sentence. Then, write the word on the board. Ask, "What do you think this word means?" Take a few suggestions and then write a definition next to the word. Explain that it is time to "bounce" to another page. Move to the second word, read the sentence that contains it, and ask students if they can guess its meaning. If they cannot, give a definition and a sample sentence. Use students' prior knowledge as a foundation for the new word. Continue bouncing through the book until the selected vocabulary words are reviewed and then read the book. If students still struggle with the words, remind them that the definitions are on the board.

Vocabulary Wall

This activity is an excellent precursor to learning to use a dictionary. From a text students will read, select three or four words that students may not understand but that are vital to comprehension. Write each word, its definition, and its phonetic spelling on a sentence strip. Explain that sometimes readers find words that they do not understand, but there is a strategy to help this problem. If readers learn those words before they read, they will comprehend the book much better. Give each student a copy of the text and help him locate the first vocabulary word. Using the sentence strips, share the word's pronunciation and definition. Then, have students use each word in a sentence. Repeat with the remaining vocabulary words, then have students create a Vocabulary Wall. Post strips in alphabetical order in a highly visible area of the classroom. Encourage students to use the Vocabulary Wall to understand new words in their reading and to use the new words in their writing. Add to the Vocabulary Wall throughout the year.

Vocabulary Guide

Explain that when people go on safaris, they may see large, exotic, dangerous animals. Tourists often hire guides to show them around and warn them about dangerous animals. Tell students that they will be guides, too. Instead of alerting visitors to big animals, they will be Vocabulary Guides to protect readers from big words. Explain that if they don't help readers, readers' understanding will be in danger. Help students find books that are at their independent reading levels. (A student reading at his level should not miss more than five words out of every 100; 10 words out of 100 is more difficult, but manageable.) If a student is unsure of more than five words in two paragraphs, she should choose another book. Give each student a Vocabulary Guide reproducible (page 14). Have students read their books, and when they find words they think might be difficult (or "dangerous") to other readers, have them write the words and page numbers on the Vocabulary Guide reproducibles. Next, have students write definitions of the words. If students are unsure of the meanings, have them ask for help. Tell students to continue reading and noting dangerous words on the reproducibles. When students have completed their books, have students use removable tape to attach their "warnings" to the fronts of the books. Place the books in the classroom library. (Group similarly leveled books in the same area.) When a student wants to read the book, she will be alerted to the large vocabulary words. As students read the books, direct them to read each dangerous word, read the definition, and go to the page where the word appears.

Make It Stick!

Each student will need one 4" by 6" (10 cm x 15 cm) sticky note for each vocabulary word. Preview a book that is part of a lesson plan and choose three or four words that will be difficult for students. Remind students that because there are so many words in the English language, they will constantly learn new words. Explain that learning new words before reading helps readers understand stories better. Distribute copies of the reading text and sticky notes. Direct students to the page where the first vocabulary word appears, then read the word and ask, "What do you think this word means?" After a few responses, share the correct definition. Have each student write the word at the top of a sticky note and write a definition in his own words. To help him remember the word, tell him to place the sticky note as close to the word as possible. Repeat with the other vocabulary words. Let students read the book and remind them that if they forget the words' meanings, they can refer to the sticky notes.

Vocabulary Guide

Write tricky words, the pages on which they appear in your book, and their definitions in the chart below.

Your book's title: _____

Word	Page	Definition

Words of the Day

Choose two vocabulary words from a current reading lesson and make two copies of the Words of the Day reproducible (page 16). Write one vocabulary word five times on one copy and write the second vocabulary word five times on the other copy. Cut out the vocabulary words. Introduce the words at the beginning of the school day. Show students the words and explain that these words will be Words of the Day. Pronounce and define each word. Display copies of the words and definitions on sentence strips in high traffic areas of the classroom—the calendar area, pencil sharpener, and doors, for example. Quiz students throughout the day. For example, on the way to recess, ask a student to define one of the words. If a student cannot define the word on the first try, have her read

the definition again. If a student asks to get a drink of water, ask for a definition before granting permission. If he can define the word, let the student get a drink. If he cannot, have the student read the definition first. Use other creative ways to have students review definitions. When it is time for the daily reading lesson, students will have been exposed to the selected vocabulary words several times. Change the Words of the Day daily, or change words weekly and have Words of the Week.

Word Illustrations

Choose three or four important and difficult vocabulary words from an upcoming reading lesson. Explain that when people know many words, others say they have "big vocabularies." Write the selected words on the board and pronounce them. Write the definition of each word on the board and use it in a sentence. Assign students to groups and give each group one vocabulary word. Have students show that they have big vocabularies by literally making the words big. Instruct each student to write his group's assigned vocabulary word as big as he can on a piece of paper. Let students make the letters "puffy" or in block style. Have each student write the definition in his own words on the paper. When everyone is finished, ask each student to read his definition to the group. Have students read their definitions again on the following day before completing the corresponding reading lesson. Note each vocabulary word as it appears in the text. Create a display by stapling the words to a bulletin board and adding the title "We Have BIG Vocabularies!"

Words of the Day

26 March

Today's word is . . .

Write a vocabulary word five times in the spaces below. Write its definition five times on sentence strips. Cut along the dashed lines. Post near high traffic areas in the classroom.

Rhyme Time

Students remember vocabulary words better when they hear them several times. Students also learn better when teachers use a variety of teaching methods. Combine both of these strategies in this activity. Select three or four words from a current reading lesson that are unfamiliar to students and important to the comprehension of the story. Write the selected vocabulary words on the board. Pronounce each word and write the definitions on the board. Then ask, "How will we remember these words?" After listening to some responses, have each student choose one word and think of a short rhyme that will help students remember the definition and pronunciation of the word. For example, if the vocabulary word is *sea anemone*, the rhyme could be, "It's a colorful creature that lives in the *sea*; it can also sting—it's an *anemone*." Explain that the vocabulary word does not have to be the word that rhymes. The vocabulary word can be in the middle of the rhyme. Let students work independently, in pairs, or in small groups. Teach the corresponding reading lesson and ask students to share their rhymes.

Word Alert!

Provide a bell for this activity. Select one or two vocabulary words from a reading, math, science, or social studies text. Remind students that when reading stories, word problems, science experiments, or even recipes, they will come across new words. Explain that it is important to learn these words because understanding words helps readers comprehend what they read. Let students take turns reading a text aloud that contains difficult but important vocabulary. There should be a follow-up lesson planned that is based on the text. Each time students encounter difficult vocabulary in the text, ring the bell. Write the difficult vocabulary words on the board, pronounce them correctly, and define them. Begin the follow-up lesson from which the vocabulary words were chosen. Students should listen and look for the vocabulary words during the lesson. When students see or hear one of these words, tell them to raise their hands and make W's (for Word Alert) with their thumbs and index fingers. Call on students who see the vocabulary words and ask them to share the meanings of the words.

Look Up for Help!

Write three vocabulary words from a reading lesson on three cards on the Look Up for Help! reproducible (page 19). Write the definitions for these words on the remaining cards and make a copy of the reproducible for each student. Have students cut out the cards. Hand out the texts (reading books, stories, etc.) that contain the vocabulary words, as well as yarn, paint stirrers, and glue. Explain that each word from the reproducible is in the text. Guide students to the page on which the first word appears. Read the sentence that contains the word and ask, "Which definition makes sense for the word in this sentence?" After listening to some responses, share the correct answer and have students glue the word cards and the matching definition cards back-to-back. Continue in the same manner for the remaining words. When the glue is dry, let students decorate the cards, making sure the words and definitions

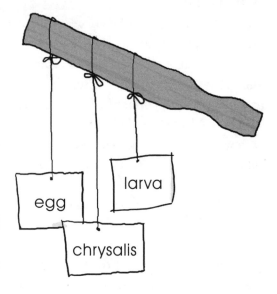

are still readable. Have students punch holes in the tops of the cards, tie pieces of yarn through the holes, and tie the other ends to paint stirrers. After all cards are attached to paint stirrers, tape the paint stirrers around the classroom so that the cards hang down. Review the vocabulary words with students and finish the original reading lesson, reminding them to look up if they need vocabulary help.

Human Thesaurus

Students understand a vocabulary word better if they can relate the word to other words they know. Explain that the reference book called a *thesaurus* helps readers find many words that mean the same thing. Give students an example. Write a sentence on the board using the word *nice*. Look up the word *nice* in a thesaurus. Read the various synonyms for the word and substitute some of the synonyms in the sentence. Then, choose three or four words from a reading lesson and write them on the board. Review each word and add its definition to the board. Ask students to think of synonyms for each word. Then, begin the reading lesson. After reading the first vocabulary word in the text, call on a "Human Thesaurus" for a synonym. Continue until synonyms have been found for all of the selected words.

First-Rate Reading™: Vocabulary • CD-104020 • © Carson-Dellosa
Basics

Look Up for Help!

Cut out the cards. Think about
what each word means. Glue the definition
to the back of the word. Punch holes in the circles, tie pieces of yarn
through the holes, and tie the other ends to a paint stirrer.

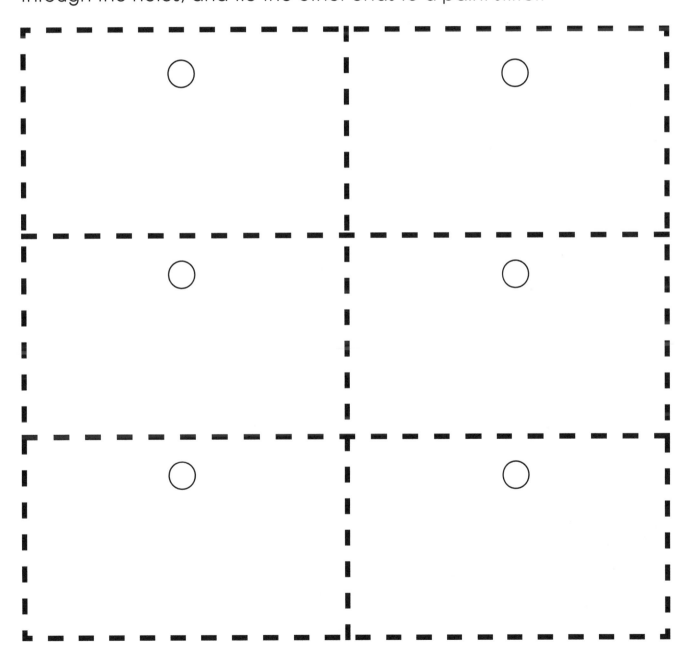

Vocabulary Hopscotch

Use chalk to draw a hopscotch outline on a sidewalk or other concrete area. Then, write a reading vocabulary word in each square of the outline. To reduce the number of vocabulary words, write *x*'s in some squares. Write all of the words, their definitions, and sample sentences on a piece of paper. Review them with students. Then, take students outside to play Vocabulary Hopscotch. Assign students to two teams. Explain that the first student on Team A should roll a die and hop the number that he rolled. If he runs out of squares, he should turn around and hop in the other direction. (Students should skip over squares with *x*'s in them.) When the student lands on a word, read the word, give a sample sentence, and read the word again. The student's team should work together to think of the word's definition. If the team is correct, they get one point. Cross out the correctly defined word on the sidewalk. If the team is wrong, the "hopper" goes to the end of the line and Team B guesses the definition of Team A's word. If Team B is correct, they get one point. Cross out the defined word, and let Team B take another turn. If Team B is incorrect, reveal the correct definition and cross out the word. Then, allow Team B to take a turn with a new word. Continue until all words have been defined. Record points on the sidewalk with chalk. The team with the most points at the end of the game wins.

Picture Dictionaries

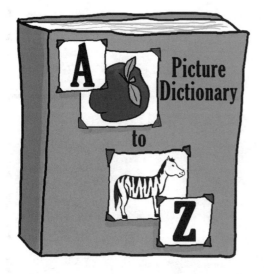

This activity allows students to create visual references of what new words mean. Choose three or four vocabulary words from a current reading lesson to write on the board. Pronounce the words and share detailed definitions. Then, assign students to groups and give each group one word. (There should be the same number of groups as vocabulary words.) Give each student a piece of paper and crayons. Show examples of children's picture dictionaries. Have each student write and illustrate a sentence using her group's vocabulary word. When students are finished, have them read their sentences and show their pictures to the rest of the group. Review the words with the class and complete the reading lesson. Alphabetize the illustrated sentences and compile into a class book titled *Our Picture Dictionary*. Repeat this activity each week and continue to add students' illustrations to the class book.

Word Tents

Select three important and difficult vocabulary words. Give each student a copy of the Word Tents reproducible (page 22), scissors, and glue. Write the first vocabulary word on the board and have each student copy it on the first section of his reproducible. Share the definition and an example sentence. Have each student write the definition in his own words beneath the word in the first section of the reproducible. Repeat with different vocabulary words in the other sections. Then, have students cut on the dashed lines and fold the papers on the solid lines. Tell each student to connect the ends by gluing the tab under the first section. The end result should look like a tent. Have students place their "word tents" on their desks. Begin reading the text, and when students hear a vocabulary word, have them turn their tents so that the appropriate vocabulary word faces them. Ask a volunteer to share the definition for that word. Continue reading and have students turn their tents as they hear the other words.

Make Way for Ducklings
title

Robert McCloskey
author

duckling   feathers   island
vocabulary words

Book Preview

Ask students, "Have you ever been to a movie? What does the theater show before the movie?" Explain that previews, or trailers (short clips of new movies that will be showing soon), are shown before the actual movies. Select three vocabulary words from a new book. Write them on the board and work with students to pronounce and define the words. Give each student a Book Preview reproducible (page 23). Have him write the book's title, the author's name, and the three vocabulary words on the appropriate lines of his reproducible. Encourage students to be creative by drawing pictures that illustrate the meanings of the words. As students finish, have each student share his book preview with a classmate. Then, read the book and stop after each vocabulary word to ask a volunteer what the word means. Create a display by stapling the book previews to a bulletin board. Add the title "Coming Soon to a Library Near You."

Word Tents

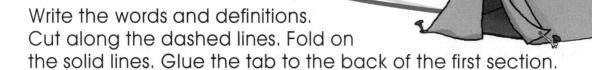

Write the words and definitions.
Cut along the dashed lines. Fold on
the solid lines. Glue the tab to the back of the first section.

Word _____

Definition _____

_____

Word _____

Definition _____

_____

Word _____

Definition _____

_____

glue

First-Rate Reading™: Vocabulary • CD-104020 • © Carson-Dellosa
Basics

Name _____

Book Preview

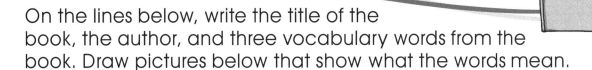

On the lines below, write the title of the book, the author, and three vocabulary words from the book. Draw pictures below that show what the words mean.

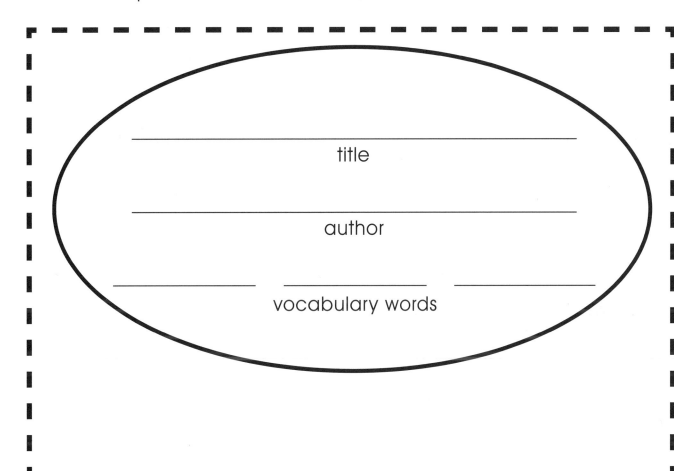

_____
title

_____
author

_____   _____   _____
vocabulary words

Brainy Bookmarks

Cut a 10" x 2" (25 cm x 5 cm) strip of light-colored construction paper for each student. (Make a few extras in case students make mistakes.) Choose a few challenging but important vocabulary words from a current reading lesson. Write one vocabulary word on the board and help students pronounce it correctly. Then, share the definition. Direct each student to write the word and its definition at the top of her strip. Repeat the process by having students add the second and third words. If students run out of room, let them write on the backs of their paper strips. Have students punch holes at the tops of their strips and attach colorful pieces of yarn to make bookmarks. When the bookmarks are complete, give each student a copy of the text and encourage students to take turns reading aloud as they use their bookmarks to track print. After each vocabulary word is read, ask a volunteer to explain what it means. If students need help, suggest that they look on their bookmarks. Let students add new words and definitions to their bookmarks throughout the school year or let them make new ones for each new book.

Vocabularians

Make two copies of the Vocabularians reproducible (page 25). Select four vocabulary words. Write each word and its definition on a badge. Explain that librarians are book experts and "vocabularians" are word experts. Then, share that four students will be vocabularians each day. Assure students that everyone will have a chance to be a word expert. Choose four students to be the day's vocabularians and give each one a badge. Have students tape their badges to their shirts or desks. During a special small group session with the day's vocabularians, write the four words on the board and share how to say them. Explain the definitions and ask these students to use the words in sentences. Then, write one of the words on each student's badge. Share with the class that these students will be experts on the words on their badges. If someone has a question about one of the four words, he should go to one of the vocabularians for help with that word. When the word appears in a book, class members should ask the vocabularian for help. If one expert isn't sure about the word, he can talk it over with another expert. Change the role of vocabularian regularly so that all students have a chance to be experts.

Name _____

Specific Word Instruction

Vocabularians

Make two copies of the reproducible. Write each vocabulary word on a badge. Give each badge to a "vocabularian" of the day.

VOCABULARIAN

VOCABULARIAN

Extended Instruction: Introduction

The more a student uses a vocabulary word, the more the word will become established in her mind. Do not just teach words one time and then abandon them for new ones. Use these activities to find ways to continue to work recently taught words into students' conversations and lessons.

Vocabulary Checklist

Choose four vocabulary words from a current reading lesson that are challenging and important to the text. Make one copy of the Vocabulary Checklist reproducible (page 27) for each student. After the reading lesson, write the vocabulary words on the board and review the pronunciations and meanings. Say, "The more you use a vocabulary word, the better you will remember it." Give each student a Vocabulary Checklist reproducible. Have each student pick one vocabulary word and write it on her checklist. Challenge students to use the words five times during the day—in conversations with friends, for example. Students can also take the lists home, use the words in conversations with family members, and return the lists the next day. Each time a student uses her word, have her write the name of the person with whom she had the conversation and the sentence that contained the word. To verify that the conversation happened, have the person with whom she spoke initial the checklist. When students have returned with the completed checklists, let them share their sentences.

Word: _____ **escape** _____

✓	sentence	initials
✓	My dog tried to escape from the fence.	AF
✓	My mom escapes into her room when she has a headache.	JW
✓	My favorite restaurant is Pizza Escape!	SL
✓	In this story, the kids help the friendly monster escape from the zoo.	EM
✓	When it's time to do chores, I can't escape from cleaning my room.	CF

Share a Word

Encourage students to be aware of whether they are comprehending what they read. Explain to students that a good reader knows when he understands a word. Help students choose books at their instructional levels. (These books should be neither frustrating nor too easy for them.) Instruct each student to write the title and author of the book on a piece of paper and then read the book. When students find words they do not know, have them copy the confusing words and their page numbers on their papers. Have students look up the words in student dictionaries and write the definitions next to the words. Then, have students reread the pages. If students find other vocabulary words they do not understand, have them use more pieces of paper to record them. After students have read for a set amount of time, collect the papers. If possible, group papers from the same books. Staple the tops of the papers to a bulletin board so that students can flip up the pages to read them. When students read new books, encourage them to look for the difficult words on the bulletin board first. Explain that looking at what others wrote about confusing words can help readers understand difficult words in the text.

First-Rate Reading™: Vocabulary • CD-104020 • © Carson-Dellosa Basics

Vocabulary Checklist

Choose a vocabulary word and write it on the line below. Your teacher will tell you how to use the checklist.

Word: _____

✓	sentence	initials

Hidden Words

Select six new words from a reading lesson that have approximately the same number of letters. Write each letter of each word on an index card and set aside the cards. Before the reading lesson, review the words with the class. Direct students to the pages in the text which include the vocabulary words. Pronounce and define the words with students. Read the story. Afterward, play a game called Hidden Words. Write the vocabulary words at the top of the board and write the definition of one word at the bottom. Place the letter cards of the matching word on the board ledge so that the blank sides face students. Assign students to two teams. Read the definition written on the board. Have students on Team A try to guess the hidden word by thinking about the definition, looking at the listed words, and counting the number of letter cards. One student from Team A should say a letter. If that letter is in the hidden word, give Team A one point, turn over the card, and let the next person on Team A guess another letter. If the student is incorrect, the first member of Team B gets to guess a letter. If he guesses correctly, give Team B one point, turn over the letter, and let the next person on Team B guess a letter. If a team chooses to guess the hidden word and is correct, that team earns a point for each hidden letter. If the team's guess is incorrect, the other team may try to guess and receive the points, or they may call out another letter. Repeat with the other five vocabulary words. The team with the most points at the end of the game is the winner. Allow the winning team to choose a book to read aloud at the end of the day.

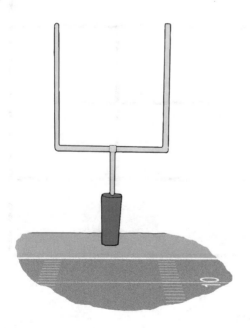

Vocabulary Bowl

Use a football analogy to make vocabulary study fun. With each reading lesson, create a list of vocabulary words from the text. Instruct students on the pronunciations and meanings of the words before, during, and after the reading lessons. After several weeks of vocabulary instruction, have a Vocabulary Bowl. Assign students to two teams and flip a coin to decide which team goes first. Read a vocabulary word and a sample sentence. Then, have Team A work together for two minutes to define the word. If Team A gives a correct definition, give them six points (like a touchdown). For an extra point, let the team members try to spell the word or give a synonym. If students give an incorrect definition, allow Team B to have a turn. Continue alternating turns. The team with the most points at the end of the game wins.

First-Rate Reading™: Vocabulary • CD-104020 • © Carson-Dellosa
Basics

Writing Folders

Students benefit from using new vocabulary words in their own writing. Encourage students to use new and different words with this activity. Choose a book that has a variety of words for the word *said,* such as *replied, whispered, exclaimed,* etc. Explain that many words mean the same thing. Using a variety of words rather than the same word repeatedly makes writing more interesting to read. Give each student a manila folder. Have her open the folder and write the word *said* on the top left corner, and underline it. Have students set aside the folders and listen to the selected reading. Direct students to raise their hands when they hear words that mean the same as *said.* When students find synonyms for *said,* write those words on the board. Review the words at the end of the story and have students write some of the words under the word *said* in their folders. Encourage students to use these synonyms instead of the word *said* in their writing. Consider allowing students to add synonyms for other overused words, such as *good, big,* and *nice,* in new columns in the same folders. Have students keep the folders accessible during reading and writing times.

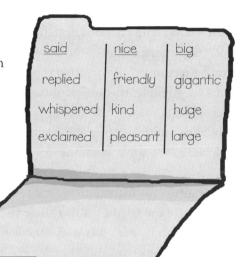

said	nice	big
replied	friendly	gigantic
whispered	kind	huge
exclaimed	pleasant	large

Same Words, Different Story

Challenge students to write stories using new vocabulary words. From a current reading lesson, choose three or four related vocabulary words that will be difficult for most students. Write the vocabulary words on the board and review their pronunciations and meanings before and during the reading lesson. After the lesson, help students brainstorm some topics that relate to the vocabulary words. Have students use these words to write their own stories. Tell students to underline the vocabulary words. When everyone is finished, schedule time for students to share their stories. Have students compare how the words are used in the original story with how they used the words in their writing. Let students staple the edges of their story pages to create books.

A Growing Vocabulary

On a large piece of paper, model how to draw a circle with five petals around it and a stem beneath it to create a flower. Write a book's title in the center of the flower. Have each student draw a similar picture on construction paper. For younger students, read a book and let them follow along in their own copies. For older students, assign them to four or five small groups and give each group multiple copies of the book. Have groups review the book and look for five words that are new or confusing to them. Tell students to write one new or confusing word on each petal. Have students use dictionaries or context clues to discover the definitions of the words. Instruct students to write each definition in a petal with its word. Let students color and cut out their flowers. When everyone is finished, have students share their words with the class. Create a display by stapling the flowers to a bulletin board and adding the title "A Growing Vocabulary."

Out of the Bag

After introducing and reviewing new vocabulary words, play Out of the Bag to help students remember them. Make two copies of the Out of the Bag reproducible (page 31). On each bag, write a vocabulary word and its definition from a previous reading lesson. Cut apart the cards and place them in a paper bag. Have one student from Team A choose one card from the bag. Team A should discuss the word and its definition. They have the option of giving the real definition or making up a definition to share with Team B. Team B should decide if the definition is true or false. If Team B guesses correctly, they get one point. If they are incorrect, they get zero points. The teams then switch roles. Continue until all of the vocabulary words are out of the bag. Throughout the year, add vocabulary words to the bag. Leave the bag and a dictionary in a center so that students can play in pairs to review important vocabulary words.

Out of the Bag

Make two copies. Write
vocabulary words and their definitions
on the cards. Cut out the cards. Place them
in a paper bag to use with the game.

Word Collections

Many students like to collect things. Ask, "Do any of you have collections at home? What would you like to add to your collections and why?" Discuss a few examples. Explain that when people collect things like rocks, stamps, or seashells, they often add things to their collections that are different from what they already have. Share that as students listen to the selected text, they need to "collect" new and different words. When a student hears a new and different word, he should raise his hand to share it with the class. Write the words on the board. Then, give each student several index cards and have her write her favorite words and definitions on the cards. If desired, have students illustrate the meanings of the words, as well. Have students share their word collections with partners. Then, read the selected text again. Ask, "Did you understand the story better when you knew what these words meant?" Continue to add interesting vocabulary words from other texts to the class word collection. Store the word cards alphabetically in an index card box. Encourage students to use words from the collection in their writing.

On the Line

On index cards, write three story vocabulary words in large print. Write the definitions of the words on the backs of the cards and set aside the cards. Write the vocabulary words on the board and explain their pronunciations and definitions. Read the story and direct students' attention to the selected vocabulary words in the text. At the end of the reading, clip each index card to a clothesline for students to access when they need reminders about the words' meanings. Repeat this procedure with several stories. When the clothesline has enough vocabulary words for the class, distribute one word to each student. Have each student write a short story that includes his word. Explain that the student may use the word several times in his writing. Tell students to underline the vocabulary words each time they use them. When students are finished, have them put the words back on the clothesline. Schedule time for students to share their stories. Have students count how many times authors used the vocabulary words in their stories. Finally, encourage students to use the vocabulary words in other independent writing.

Vocabulary Hoops

Choose words that students are familiar with to complete the Vocabulary Hoops reproducible (page 34). Copy the reproducible and cut out the cards. Number the backs of the cards and write the answers on a separate piece of paper. Tape the cards on the board so that the numbers are showing. Assign students to two teams. Have Team A choose a number from the board. Read the selected question and give Team A time to answer it. If Team A answers correctly, give them the card. It is then Team B's turn. If Team A answers incorrectly, allow Team B to share their answer for Team A's question. If Team B is correct, they get the card. If Team B is incorrect, the card goes in a discard pile and should be further reviewed. A member from Team B should choose a number from the remaining cards. Each card is worth two points. Each time either team receives a card, allow students to exclaim "SWOOSH!" one time. Repeat the process until there are no cards on the board. The team with the most cards at the end of the game wins. Encourage good sportsmanship. Rather than emphasizing the winner, set a class goal that both teams can work together to reach. If the class is able to answer all questions correctly two weeks in a row, for example, allow some time for the class to play basketball as a reward.

Word Hunt

Fill in the blanks on the Word Hunt reproducible (page 35) with clues to vocabulary words found in the classroom or the school's environmental print. When the reproducible is complete, make a class set. Have students go on a scavenger hunt for words. Pair nonreaders with readers for the hunt. Set and explain the boundaries for where students can go to find the words. Give each student a copy of the Word Hunt reproducible. Read each sentence to make sure students understand the words before they look for them. After a given amount of time, let students share their answers to the questions. Survey the class to see if any students found all of the words. For added challenge and motivation, have pairs of students design word hunts for other pairs of students. Let those going on the word hunt use an instant or digital camera to take pictures of the appropriate words. Use the photos to check students' findings, then have the pairs switch roles.

Vocabulary Hoops

Complete the questions below.
Cut out the cards and use them to play
Vocabulary Hoops.

What does the word

_____ mean?

What word starts with the letter

_____ and means _____

_____

_____?

What is a _____ -syllable word

that means the same as _____

_____

_____?

How do you pronounce this

word? (Write the word on the

board.)

What does a _____

look like?

What do you use a _____

_____ for?

How do you spell the word

_____?

Where do you find a

_____?

First-Rate Reading™: Vocabulary • CD-104020 • © Carson-Dellosa
Basics

Word Hunt

Look at the vocabulary clues.
Answer as many questions as you can.

1. Find a word that means _____.
   Write the word and where you found it here: _____

   _____

2. Find a poster that has the word _____
   on it. Write where you found the poster here: _____

3. Find a word that has _____ syllables or beats. Write the word here:

   _____

4. Find a book that has the word _____
   in the title. Record the title of the book here:

   _____

5. Find a word that has _____ letters and ends with _____ . Write the
   word here: _____

6. Find something that is _____.
   Write the name of the object here: _____

7. Find something that has _____.
   Write the word here: _____

Vocabulary Concentration

Select six new vocabulary words from a reading lesson. The words should be important to the meaning of the text. Write them on the board and explain that they are part of a current reading lesson. Read the words and share the definitions. After the reading lesson, give students more practice with the vocabulary words. Assign partners, give each pair of students 12 index cards, and have pairs work together to write the vocabulary words on six of the cards, and the definitions on the remaining six cards. Have students play Vocabulary Concentration. Partners should turn cards facedown, mix them up, and place the cards in rows between them. Have students take turns turning over two cards at a time to try to find a match. If the cards match, the student should keep the two cards and take another turn. If the word and definition do not match, the player should turn over the cards and play moves to the next player. Partners should take turns until all cards are gone. The player with the most cards at the end of the game wins.

Friendship Story

Remind students that stories are more interesting when writers use a variety of words. When a writer uses the same words over and over again, the story gets boring. Make two copies of the Friendship Story reproducible (page 37), which describes kids playing in a park. Have students suggest words for the blanks in the Friendship Story. Tell students what kinds of words are needed to fill in the blanks, but do not read the surrounding sentences. For example, one blank reads *another word for said*. Students may suggest *whispered, answered,* or *shouted.* Write a suggestion on the line and continue filling in the blanks with student suggestions. Encourage students to be as creative as possible. Before reading the text to the class, repeat the process with the other copy. The second time through, ask students to supply different words. After filling in all blanks a second time, read the first version and then read the second version. Have students compare the paragraphs. Ask, "How different are the two stories? Which one do you like better? Why?" Encourage students to notice whether authors use a variety of words in their writing.

Friendship Story

Make two copies. Have students
suggest words to match the clues in parentheses.
Record their responses and repeat on the other copy.
Read both versions.

One sunny afternoon, two _____ went to the park and saw
(another word for friends)

a boy sitting by himself. He leaned his head on one of the chains as he

quietly sat in a swing. _____ _____, "Let's see if
(first friend's name)   (another word for said)

he wants to play with us." _____ asked her grandpa, who
(second friend's name-female)

had brought them to the park, if they could walk over to the swing set.

He agreed and walked with them. _____ said, "_____.
(first friend's name)   (another word for hello)

I _____ playing _____. Do you want to play, too?"
(another word for like)   (name of game)

He nodded, and they ran off to play. After playing a game of

_____, _____ announced, "You are so _____
(same game)   (second friend's name)   (another word for good)

at _____." The little boy smiled and _____ to meet
(same game)   (another word for walked)

his mother who was watching them by a tree. "See you next time!"

_____ _____.
(another word for said)   (first friend's name)

Round of Applause

Choose five vocabulary words from a reading lesson and write them on the board. Teach students the pronunciations and definitions for the words. Read the text that includes the selected vocabulary words. Give each student two different-colored pieces of construction paper and have her trace the same hand on each piece of paper. Have each student write one vocabulary word on each finger of one hand, keeping the hands turned so that the thumbs are pointed in the same direction. Then, let students think about the definitions of the words. If students cannot remember them, allow students to look at the book or use dictionaries. Have each student write one definition on each finger of the other hand. The same fingers on both hands should have matching words and definitions. For example, if the word *fuchsia* is written on the thumb, the definition for *fuchsia* should be written on the thumb of the second hand. Create a display of the paper hands. Place the hands on top of each other so that the thumbs and fingers line up as if the hands are clapping. Rotate one hand in each pair so that both words and definitions are visible. Staple the pairs of hands in a circle (or circles) on the bulletin board and add the title "A Round of Applause for New Words."

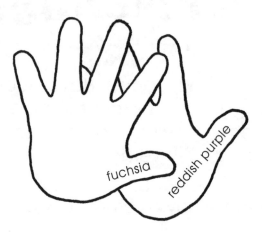

Understanding Idioms

Part of vocabulary instruction is playing with words. Students at first- and second-grade reading levels can learn about word play by reading and understanding idioms. Explain that idioms are figures of speech. Explain that these phrases are not literal. For example, share that to *see eye to eye with someone* doesn't mean that two people are looking into each other's eyes. The phrase means that people agree with each other. Explain that to be *on the ball* does not mean someone is sitting on a ball. *On the ball* means able to get things done. Read *Amelia Bedelia* by Peggy Parrish (HarperCollins, 1983) to provide students with more exposure to idioms. In order to understand what they are reading, readers need to understand idioms they see in texts. Read the idioms on the Understanding Idioms reproducible (page 39) and explain what each one means. Give each student an idiom from the reproducible and have him illustrate the correct meaning. Distribute paper, markers, and glue. After students have drawn pictures on their papers, have them glue the idioms to the pictures. When everyone is finished, have students show their pictures and explain their idioms.

Understanding Idioms

Use this page with the
Understanding Idioms activity (page 38).
Make enough copies for each student to have one idiom.
Cut out and give one sentence to each student.

1. If you have a sweet tooth, you love to eat sweet things like candy.

2. To butter someone up is to say very nice things so that he will do something for you.

3. If someone drives you crazy, his behavior really bothers you.

4. If someone says, "Go fly a kite," she is telling you to go away.

5. If your head is in the clouds, you are probably daydreaming.

6. To get up on the wrong side of bed is to wake up grouchy.

7. To keep something under your hat is to keep a secret.

8. If you are on cloud nine, you are very happy.

9. If someone is pulling your leg, she is fooling you.

10. On the double means very quickly, as in double the speed.

Using Reference Aids: Introduction

Remind students that not understanding words affects their reading comprehension. Explain that dictionaries and glossaries are reference aids that list words alphabetically to help readers find words and their meanings quickly. Explain that because a word sometimes has multiple meanings, students will need to read each meaning and think about the context in which the word is used in order to choose the correct definition.

Easy as ABC

The first skill in learning how to use a dictionary is understanding alphabetical order. Give students the basics with this lesson. Write each letter of the alphabet on a separate piece of paper. If there are more than 26 students in the class, duplicate some letters. If there are fewer than 26 students, consider writing two consecutive letters on a page. Explain that there are many different ways to put things in order. In a dictionary, words are listed in the same sequence as the letters of the alphabet. Have students review alphabetical (ABC) order. Give each student a letter and have him tape it to his shirt. Ask, "What letter of the alphabet comes first?" Ask the student wearing the letter A to come to the front of the classroom. Then say, "What letter comes after A in the alphabet?" Direct the student wearing the B to stand next to the student with the A. Continue with the rest of the letters in the alphabet. If there are duplicate letters, have students wearing the same letters stand behind each other. After everyone is standing, mix up students and challenge them to put themselves in alphabetical order.

Alphabet Race

After introducing students to the concept of alphabetical order, review the alphabet. Explain that to put words in alphabetical order, students must look at the first letters of the words, then put them in the same order as they appear in the alphabet. Write the words *bike, ant, dip,* and *cut* on the board. Ask, "Which word comes first in a dictionary?" Write the answer (*ant*), on a different part of the board. Say, "Which word comes after *ant*?" Add the word *bike* after *ant*. Continue asking what word is next. Explain that sometimes letters are skipped. (For example, you may have a word that begins with the letter *a*, a word that begins with *b*, and a word that begins with *d*, but no word that begins with *c*, so the letter *c* is skipped.) Write the words *mug, dog, fast,* and *sell* on the board. Work with students to put the words in alphabetical order. Then, give each student a copy of the Alphabet Race reproducible (page 41). Have students cut out the cards and place them in alphabetical order. (Have the alphabet posted in the classroom for reference.) When students are finished, review the answers. Then, challenge the class to a race. Have each student mix up his set of words. When you say "go," have students put the words back in alphabetical order as fast as they can. When each student has alphabetized his words, have him put his hands on his head. Check the order as students finish. Answer Key: *apple, book, clock, door, frog, keys, lion, pen,* and *sun.*

Word-Learning Strategies

Alphabet Race

Cut out the cards.
Put the words in ABC (alphabetical) order.

pen

apple

sun

frog

keys

lion

door

clock

book

Name Order

When students understand alphabetical order, ask, "How do you put words in alphabetical order when there is more than one word that begins with the letter *a*? How will we find it among the other *a* words?" Explain that when two words begin with the same letter, students must look at the second letters. The words can then be put in alphabetical order according to the second letters. Write the following words on the board: *ask, add, am,* and *all.* Have a volunteer circle the second letter in each word. Tell students, "Because the beginning letter is the same in all four words, we need to look at the second letter in each word to put the words in alphabetical order. When looking at the second letters (*s, d, m,* and *l*), which one comes first in the alphabet?" Write the word *add* on the board. Then, ask, "Which of the remaining letters (*s, m,* and *l*) comes next in the alphabet?" Write the word *all* after the word *add.* Continue with the other words. Summarize by saying, "When alphabetizing words, look at the beginning letter first to put the words in alphabetical order. If two or more words begin with the same letter, go to the second letters to alphabetize. If the first two letters are the same, then look at the third letters, and so on." Have each student write her first name on a sentence strip. Tell students to place their names in alphabetical order. Begin by having students whose names begin with A stand at the front of the classroom with their sentence strips. If there is more than one student whose name begins with A, work with the class to alphabetize according to the next letters. Repeat until all students are in order, then call up small groups of students for the class to alphabetize.

Word Guides

In this activity, have 12 students act as dictionary guides while other students alphabetize words. Write *act, dust, each, hut, ice, lunch, mad, put, quack, tug, umbrella,* and *zoom* on separate pieces of paper. On index cards, write *bell, can, dog, eel, fox, gate, jump, kite, lap, mug, nest, off, rock, sat, top, van, we,* and *you.* Explain that dictionaries have guide words at the top of each page. Show a page from a dictionary. Tell students that guide words show the first and last words on the page. Just by looking at the guide words on a page, a reader can tell if the word he is looking for is listed on that page. Give 12 students one guide word each. Have these students stand next to each other in the order listed below. Distribute the index cards to the remaining students. Help students place each word between the two students holding the appropriate guide words. For example, if a student holds the word *bell,* he should stand between students holding the words *act* and *dust.* When each word is between its guide words, review answers with the class. Following are the answers:

- Between the guide words *act* and *dust,* students should place the words *bell, can,* and *dog.*
- Between the guide words *each* and *hut,* students should place the words *eel, fox,* and *gate.*
- Between the guide words *ice* and *lunch,* students should place the words *jump, kite,* and *lap.*
- Between the guide words *mad* and *put,* students should place the words *mug, nest,* and *off.*
- Between the guide words *quack* and *tug,* students should place the words *rock, sat,* and *top.*
- Between the guide words *umbrella* and *zoom,* students should place the words *van, we,* and *you.*

Guide-ing Instruction

Gather six pieces of chart paper. At the top of each piece of chart paper, write a pair of the following guide words: *bad–bog, bone–by, pack–pie, pig–put, sad–seed,* and *seem–sun.* Tape the pieces of chart paper around the room and place a tape dispenser near each piece. Write the words *bag, bat, bed, bit, boat, book, box, bug, bus, buzz, pad, pat, peel, peg, pen, pill, pit, pop, puff, push, safe, sand, sap, sat, sea, set, side, sip, six,* and *so* on index cards. Give each student one word. Review alphabetical order and the concept of guide words. Remind students that when they use dictionaries, they should look at the guide words and think about alphabetical order to find out what page a word is on. Show students how to go to the letter first and then use the guide words to find the correct page. Give students time for independent practice with finding correct dictionary pages and placing words in alphabetical order. Next, give each student a word on an index card and explain that the pieces of chart paper around the room are pretend dictionary pages. Have each student walk around to find the page where her word would be in a dictionary. For example, if a student's word is *sand* she should go to the *sad/seed* page because her word should be listed between *sad* and *seed.* When students have found their pages, have them work together to alphabetize the words on each page. Have students tape their words to the pages in alphabetical order. When the groups are finished, review the answers with the class. Answer Key = bad–bog: bag, bat, beg, bit, boat; bone–by: book, box, bug, bus, buzz; pack–pie: pad, pat, peel, peg, pen; pig–put: pill, pit, pop, puff, push; sad–seed: safe, sand, sap, sat, sea; seem–sun: set, side, sip, six, so

Guide Word Dictionary

Remind students of why each dictionary page has two guide words. Give each student a copy of the Guide Word Dictionary reproducible (page 44). Have students write the words from the Word List in alphabetical order under the guide words. Direct students to cut out the pages (including the cover page), place them in order, and staple the pages together. To extend the activity, make additional word lists throughout the year. Give students copies of blank Guide Word Dictionary book pages and allow them to create new dictionaries with the word lists you have created. As an extra challenge, make a master list of the words you have used throughout the year for this activity and challenge students to alphabetize all of them. Write each word on an index card and place the cards at a center with an answer key, or post the cards on a bulletin board and alphabetize them in small groups or as a whole class. Answer Key = Page 1: bird, cave, dig; Page 2: fell, gum, hot; Page 3: lamp, my, nine; Page 4: rag, see, tan; Page 5: vine, won, zip

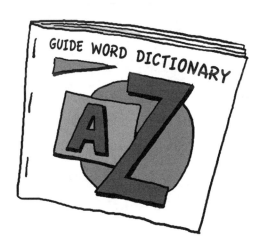

Name _____ *Word-Learning Strategies*

Guide Word Dictionary

Copy the words from the list onto the pages.
Use the guide words to make sure the words from the list are in ABC order. Cut out the pages. Staple them together to make a book.

GUIDE WORD DICTIONARY

A Z

ant	elf
fast	jog
kick	over
pat	tub
under	zoo

Word List:

tan
bird
see
cave
nine
fell
gum
dig
hot
lamp
my
rag
zip
won
vine

44

First-Rate Reading™: Vocabulary Basics • CD-104020 • © Carson-Dellosa

Class Pronunciation Guide

On index cards, write the following words: *great, because, field, why, night, no, low, few, batch, know, away, write, foot, book, ball, ago, knit, beauty, light, fly, city, wrist, is, was, happy, what, day, knee, climb,* and *snow.* Give each student a word. Assign shorter words, such as *is* and *was,* to struggling students and give more proficient readers words such as *because* and *beauty.* Explain that sometimes words do not sound like they look. Write the word *menu* on the board. Tell students that if they were unsure what the word was, they might pronounce the word *men-uh.* However, the real pronunciation is *men-yu.* Write *men-yu* in parentheses after the word *menu.* Explain that the "word" in parentheses is a pronunciation guide—it helps people know how to say the word. Give each student one word on a sentence strip and have him read it. Then, instruct students to write the way the words really sound in parentheses after the words. Do not worry about specific pronunciation codes or symbols at this point; just have students write words phonetically. When students are finished, ask them to share their words and pronunciation guides. Create a display with students' pronunciation guides. Place the words in alphabetical order on a bulletin board and add the title "Class Pronunciation Guide."

Code Cracker

Make one copy of the Code Cracker reproducible (page 46) for each student. Provide a dictionary for each student. Explain that pronunciation guides in dictionaries use different codes to explain how to read words. The "code cracker" will help students read the codes. Tell students that to use pronunciation guides, they should first look up a word using its correct spelling. Write the word *decide* on the board and have students find it in their dictionaries. Remind students that the pronunciation guide is after the word, and it has a dash or dot between each chunk (or syllable). Work with students to use the "code cracker" to decode each chunk. Have students look up other vocabulary words. (Use only words with short or long vowel sounds, and note that some dictionaries do not use symbols to show short vowels.) Encourage students to use the "code cracker" and dictionary to read each word. Tell students that eventually, they will not need the "code cracker" for pronunciation help with these words.

Code Cracker

Vowel sounds are often either short or long. Dictionaries show how to pronounce vowels in different ways.

Short vowels

Some dictionaries use symbols to show how to pronounce short vowels. Symbol in Pronunciation Guide: a curved line over a vowel, or no symbol

Examples: short a = (ă) as in *sat* (săt)

short e = (ĕ) as in *best* (bĕst)

short i = (ĭ) as in *pig* (pĭg)

short o = (ŏ) as in *hop* (hŏp)

short u = (ŭ) as in *rug* (rŭg)

Long vowels

Some dictionaries use symbols to show how to pronounce long vowels. Symbol in Pronunciation Guide: a straight line over a vowel

Examples: long a = (ā) as in *rain* (rān)

long e = (ē) as in *eat* (ēt)

long i = (ī) as in *night* (nīt)

long o = (ō) as in *rope* (rōp)

long u = (ū) as in *you* (yū)

Other ways to show vowels and consonants

Sometimes dictionaries show how to pronounce vowels and consonants by spelling the words differently.

Examples: city = (si-tee)

cute = (kyoot)

easy = (ee-zee)

itch = (ich)

daisy = (day-zee)

First-Rate Reading™: Vocabulary • CD-104020 • © Carson-Dellosa
Basics

Syllable Stress

Many dictionaries indicate which syllable in a word is stressed. Some dictionaries use bold type to indicate a stressed syllable while others place an accent mark before or after a stressed syllable. These marks can be confusing to students, so help them discover how dictionaries show stress. Choose a simple word for students to look up, such as *better*. Say the word with the correct stress, then say it with stress on the second syllable. Ask students to listen to you say it, then tell you which syllable should have more emphasis (the first). Have students look up *better* in dictionaries and tell you what they notice about the first syllable. It should either be in bold type or have an accent mark. Explain that this tells you which syllable to stress. Then, choose another word to say, such as *alone*. Again, say the word with stress on the first and then on the second syllable. Tell students not to call out the answer but to guess silently which syllable should be stressed. When students have made their silent guesses, have them look up the word in dictionaries and decide whether their guesses are correct. Ask a volunteer to reveal his guess, tell whether it matches what the dictionary shows, and describe how he knows which syllable the dictionary shows to stress. Repeat for other words, then let individual students choose words for the class to guess.

Look It Up

Empower students with the skills to say and understand words. Select five vocabulary words from a current reading lesson that will be difficult for students to pronounce. Write the selected words on the board. Give each student a dictionary or have students share dictionaries. Direct students to use the dictionaries to find the first word on the board. Ask students to use the pronunciation guide to decode the word. Ask, "How do you say this word? What does this word mean?" Work with students to read the definition. Write it on the board and continue with the rest of the words. Leave dictionaries in the classroom library so that students can continue to look up words during their independent reading or writing time.

Which Definition?

Choose five vocabulary words from a reading lesson that have multiple meanings. On the board, draw a chart with six rows and three columns. Write the headings *Vocabulary*, *Word in a Sentence*, and *Definition* at the top of the chart. Write the vocabulary words under the *Vocabulary* heading, then write sentences that contain the vocabulary words and context clues in the center column. (Use sentences from the reading or make up new ones, if necessary.) Underline the vocabulary word in each sentence. Leave the *Definition* column blank. Explain that dictionaries are great tools for finding vocabulary words, but sometimes there is more than one definition for a word. If there is more than one definition, students should read the sentence and see which definition makes sense in the sentence. Have students use dictionaries to look up the first underlined word, read the different definitions, then reread the sentence on the chart. Have students vote on which definition they think is correct. Reveal the answer, then write the correct definition in the third column on the chart. Use the same procedure for the remaining vocabulary words.

Silly Sentences

Select four or five vocabulary words from a reading lesson that have multiple meanings. Make a note about the location of the words in the dictionaries students will be using so that you can find them easily, then distribute the dictionaries to students. Have students use them to find the meanings of the selected words. Begin the reading lesson. After reading one of the selected vocabulary words, read the rest of the sentence and stop. Have students look up the word in the dictionaries. Then, have volunteers read the various definitions. Say, "This word has more than one definition. How will we know which one is the correct definition? Let's try substituting the meaning for the word." "Think aloud" and choose the definition that would not make sense in the sentence. For example, if the vocabulary word is *ball* and the sentence is, "The princess wore a beautiful gown to the ball," *ball* is obviously a dance in this case. But, there are several definitions for the word *ball. Ball* can also mean a round object to use in a game. If using the second meaning in the sentence, the princess might be walking in the direction of a sports ball. Ask, "Does that make sense?" Continue substituting definitions in the sentence until students find the correct definition for the word. Repeat the process throughout the reading lesson until students have looked up definitions for all of the selected vocabulary words.

Find and Define

Have each student choose a book that is a little difficult. The book should have some unknown words but not more than 10 difficult words per 100. Give each student a copy of the Find and Define reproducible (page 49). Tell each student to skim the book and look for difficult words. When each student finds an unfamiliar word, have her write it on the reproducible. Have her record the page number on which she found the word. Let students look up the unfamiliar words in dictionaries, then write the correct definitions on their reproducibles. If students must choose between multiple definitions, instruct them to reread the sentences containing the words and think about their meanings. Then, have them choose definitions that make sense. When students have found most of the difficult vocabulary words, have them review the definitions and finish reading their books. Encourage students to use this word-learning strategy during independent reading time.

First-Rate Reading™: Vocabulary • CD-104020 • © Carson-Dellosa
Basics

Find and Define

Skim a book. Write unknown words
and the page numbers on which you found them.
Look up the words in a dictionary and write the definitions.

Book title: _____

1. New word: _____   Page Number: _____

    Definition: _____

    _____

2. New word: _____   Page Number: _____

    Definition: _____

    _____

3. New word: _____   Page Number: _____

    Definition: _____

    _____

4. New word: _____   Page Number: _____

    Definition: _____

    _____

5. New word: _____   Page Number: _____

    Definition: _____

    _____

Star Words

For this activity, supply a hole punch, yarn, and a book or a chapter in a book about space that has a glossary. Explain that sometimes books have a little dictionary in the back that is called a *glossary*. Point out that some words in the book are in bold print; share that those words are probably defined in the glossary. Select three words from the book's glossary. Give each student a few copies of a star pattern on light-colored paper and read the book or chapter to the class. When reading one of the vocabulary words, write it on the board. Have each student write that word on a star. Then, explain that the words in the glossary are listed in alphabetical order like they are in a dictionary. Ask a volunteer to find the word in the glossary and read the definition to the class. Have each student turn over his star and write the definition in his own words on the back. Repeat with the remaining vocabulary words. After finishing the book, ask, "What is a glossary? How do you find words in a glossary?" Let students cut out the stars, punch holes in the tops, thread pieces of yarn through the holes, and tie the yarn. Hang the stars from the ceiling, in doorways, in front of windows, or from students' desks. Treat vocabulary words from other books the same way. For example, use hearts for a book about Valentine's Day, fish shapes for a book about the ocean, etc.

Class Glossary

Every teacher uses certain phrases to describe classroom routines. At the end of a day, some teachers say, "Stack and pack," meaning that it is time for students to stack their chairs and pack their bags. A new student may not be familiar with his teacher's terms. Help new students by creating a class glossary. Have students brainstorm expressions or phrases used in class, such as, "One, two, three, eyes on me." Record students' responses on the board. Have students choose four phrases from the board and define each one on a Class Glossary reproducible (page 51). Consider having students illustrate the phrases on the backs of the reproducibles. Place reproducibles at the back of a class book about students or a typical day at school. Read the book when new students arrive in the classroom. Add to the class glossary as needed throughout the year.

Class Glossary

Choose four phrases from the board to write and define.

1. Phrase: _____

   Definition: _____

   _____

2. Phrase: _____

   Definition: _____

   _____

3. Phrase: _____

   Definition: _____

   _____

4. Phrase: _____

   Definition: _____

   _____

Word Parts: Introduction

Understanding contractions, compound words, prefixes, and suffixes helps readers understand words and their meanings. This section provides activities that help students recognize and analyze word parts.

Contraction Math

Write the following on the board:

it + is = _____   what + is = _____

she + is = _____   he + is = _____

we + are = _____   you + are = _____

they + are = _____

Tell students that a contraction is a shorter way of writing two words and that contractions can only be made with certain words. Tell students that contractions are like math. In math, two numbers are added together to make another number. With contractions, two words are added together to make another word. Go to the first "problem." Write the contraction *it's* on the line. Explain that when *it* and *is* are added together, they equal the contraction *it's*. *It is* and *it's* mean the same thing. *It's* is just a shorter way of writing *it is*. Point out that the letter *i* in *is* was replaced with an *apostrophe*. Explain that an apostrophe looks like a comma but is placed higher. Move to the next problem and share that the words *what* and *is* can be combined to form the contraction *what's*. Write the contraction *what's* on the line. Ask for volunteers to write contractions for the remaining problems. Review answers with the class. To reinforce that a contraction and its words mean the same thing, have students substitute one for the other in a sentence. Erase the board and give each student a Contraction Math reproducible (page 53). After students have finished the problems, review the answers.

Character Predictions

Choose an unfamiliar book that has a male character and a female character. Explain that there is a shorter way to write and say the words *he* and *will*. Write the words *he will* on the board. Share that to make a contraction with the word *will*, students should replace the letters *wi* with an apostrophe and "squish" *he* and *ll* together. Write *he'll* on the board. Tell students that *he will* and *he'll* mean the same thing. Write the words *she* and *will* on the board. Work with students to make the contraction *she'll*. Do the same for *I will* and *I'll*. Give each student a copy of the Character Predictions reproducible (page 54). Show students the book cover and tell them there is a male character in the book. Have students predict what the male character will do and begin their predictions with the contraction *he'll*. Then, show the female character and have students make predictions using the contraction *she'll*. Lastly, have students write whether they think they will like the story. They should begin their sentences with *I'll* and explain the reasoning behind their predictions. Finally, read the selected text. After listening to the story, have students assess their predictions.

Contraction Math

Replace the first letter in each
second word with an apostrophe. "Squish"
the two chunks together to make each contraction.

I. you + are = _____

2. they + are= _____

3. he + is= _____

4. she + is= _____

5. we + are= _____

6. it + is= _____

Use the answers above to fill in the blanks below.

_____ learning about contractions. _____ shorter
       I.   2.

ways to write pairs of words. If a boy is going to school, you could say,

" _____ going to school." If a girl is playing soccer, you
      3.

could say, "_____ playing soccer." If your mother asks you
        4.

what your class is learning at school, you could say, "_____
                                             5.

learning about contractions. _____ so much fun!"
                              6.

Character Predictions

What's going to happen next?

Use the contractions *he'll, she'll,* and *I'll* to answer the questions on the lines below.

What do you think the male character will do?

_____

_____

_____

What do you think the female character will do?

_____

_____

_____

Do you think you will like the story?

_____

_____

_____

Contractions with Not

For this activity, give each student an erasable board, a write-on/wipe-away marker or chalk, and an index card. If erasable boards are not available, students may use paper and pencils. Write the contraction *didn't* on the board and explain that *didn't* means *did not*. Write the following sentences on the board and read them: *He didn't do his homework. He did not do his homework.* Ask, "Do these two sentences mean the same thing?" The contraction did not (or didn't) change the meaning of the sentence. Write the words *did not* below the contraction *didn't*. Explain that to make the contraction *didn't*, the *o* was replaced with an apostrophe and the letters were "squished" together. (Remind students how to make an apostrophe. Explain that it looks like a high comma.) Explain that not all words can be part of contractions, but contractions with the word *not* are very common. Have each student write the word *not* on an index card. Then, write the word *wasn't* on the board. Have students copy the contraction on their erasable boards. Explain that the word *wasn't* is a contraction; they can tell it's a contraction because of the apostrophe. Share a simple sentence using the word *wasn't*. Then, have students place their index cards over the *n't* part of the word on their erasable boards. Ask, "What two words make up the contraction *wasn't*?" Repeat with the words *doesn't*, *hadn't*, *isn't*, *weren't*, *shouldn't*, and *couldn't*.

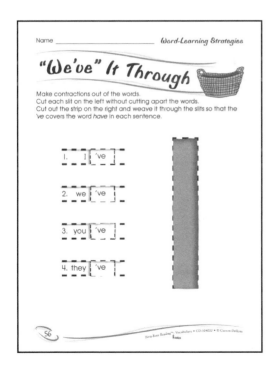

"We've" It Through

Remind students that a contraction is a short version of two combined words. Explain that the word *have* can be used to make contractions. Write the words *we* and *have* on the board. Tell students that the contraction for *we have* is *we've*. Write *we've* on the board and share that the first two letters in *have* disappeared and have been replaced with an apostrophe. Tell students that *we have* and *we've* mean the same thing. *We've* is just a shorter way to say *we have*. Give each student a copy of the "We've" It Through reproducible (page 56). Tell students to cut out the *'ve* strip. Then, show how to cut slits on each of the dotted lines around the numbered words. Work with students to read each pair of words (*I have*, *we have*, etc.). Let each student change the words into contractions by pushing the *'ve* strip through the slits. Have each student pull the strip so that *'ve* covers the word *have* in each instance. Help students read each contraction and use it in a sentence.

"We've" It Through

Make contractions out of the words.
Cut each slit on the left without cutting apart the phrases.
Cut out the strip on the right and weave it through the slits so that the
've covers the word *have* in each phrase.

1.   I   have

2. we   have

3. you   have

4. they   have

've

've

've

've

First-Rate Reading™ Vocabulary • CD-104020 • © Carson-Dellosa
Basics

Beginnings and Endings

Provide two colors of index cards. On one color, write *after, any, back, base, bee, bird, blue, butter, camp, earth, foot, jelly,* and *sail.* On the other color, write *noon, thing, pack, ball, hive, house, berry, fly, fire, quake, print, fish,* and *boat.* Write only one word on each card. Explain that a *compound word* is made up of two smaller words. Write the compound word *earthquake* on the board and draw a slash between *earth* and *quake.* Tell students that *earthquake* is a compound word because it is made up of two smaller words—*earth* and *quake.* Explain that a good strategy for reading compound words is to look for the smaller words first, then read the two smaller words together to get the compound word. Show students the words on the cards and explain that the words on the first color of cards are the beginning parts of compound words. The words on the other color of cards are the ending parts of compound words. Share that each card has a match that is a different color; the two words together make a compound word. Give each student one card. Make sure students understand that if they have one color of card, their partners will have the other color. Note that a few words have more than one match, such as *foot, blue,* and *butter.* Give students one minute to find their partners. When students find their partners, have each pair place the cards together to read the word. If the two words make a compound word, students have a match. If the two words do not make a compound word, students must find new partners. Check students' matches to make sure everyone has an appropriate partner. When students match their cards, tell them to write sentences using their compound words.

Compound Word Rainbow

Write the compound word *rainbow* on the board. Draw a slash between the words *rain* and *bow.* Share that *rainbow* is a compound word because it is made up of two smaller words—*rain* and *bow.* Remind students that a good way to read a compound word is to find the two smaller words and read them. Give each student a copy of the Compound Word Rainbow reproducible (page 58), colored pencils, and a marker. Let each student choose three compound words from the Compound Word list on the reproducible. Instruct each student to use his marker to write a sentence using one compound word in each section of the rainbow. Have students color each section and cut out their rainbows. Allow time for them to share their sentences. Staple the rainbows to a bulletin board and add the title "A Rainbow of Compound Words."

Compound Word Rainbow

Choose four compound words
from the list below. Write a sentence using
one compound word on each line of the rainbow.
The first one is done for you.

I put the letter in the mailbox.

Compound Word List:
rainbow, mailbox,
lunchroom, popcorn,
starfish, waterfall,
toolbox, sunshine,
motorcycle, peanut

Compound Riddles

Write the words *armchair, basketball, birdbath, bullfrog, clothespin, cookbook, cowboy, cupcake, dragonfly, eyeball, fingernail, firefly, football, mailman, moonlight, pancake, pinwheel, playpen, popcorn, raincoat, sandpaper, sidewalk, snowman, sunflower, toenail, toothbrush,* and *watchdog* on separate pieces of paper. Review any unfamiliar words. Write the word *butterfly* on the board. Draw a slash between the words *butter* and *fly* and ask students to read *butterfly.* Explain that sometimes compound words mean what they sound like—*homework* is work at home—but sometimes they don't. Ask, "Is a butterfly really made out of butter? What would a fly made of butter look like?" Draw what students suggest. Give each student a compound word and a piece of paper. Instruct each student to look for the two smaller words in the compound word and let students think of silly (and literal) ways to draw what their compound words mean. For example, if a student has the word *cupcake* she could draw a cake in a teacup. Have students draw pictures on one side of the papers and write the compound words on the backs of the papers. When students are finished, collect the pictures and assemble them in a class book titled *Our Compound Word Riddles.* Show the pictures and have students guess each other's compound words.

Compound Clubhouse

Cover a clean, paper milk or orange juice carton with brown paper to resemble a miniature house. Add a sign to the door that says Compound Clubhouse. Explain that *clubhouse* is a compound word because it has two smaller words in it. The smaller words are words that make sense by themselves in sentences. For example, "She loved reading, so she joined the book *club.* I think the book club meets every week at Jasmine's *house.*" Tell students that a new club, the "Compound," is meeting in the classroom, and everyone is invited to be a member. Explain that to join the club, each student must be able to read 10 compound words. Let students search around the classroom for compound words. Remind students that they will have to make sure their words are compound by finding the two smaller words in each. When each student thinks he has found 10 compound words, have him practice reading the words with a classmate and then read them to you. If he reads the words correctly, write his name on a small piece of paper and staple it to the clubhouse. Continue adding names to the "clubhouse" when students pass the "membership test."

Guess My Definition

Explain that a *prefix* is a word chunk at the beginning of a word that affects the word's meaning. Share that looking at prefixes helps readers understand words. Write the word *unable* on the board. Draw a line under the prefix *un-* and share that *un-* is a prefix that means *the opposite of* or *not*. When *un-* appears in front of the root word *able*, this word means *not able*. Give students an example, such as "I'm *unable* to go to your party." Explain that the sentence means, "I cannot go to your party." Have students play a game called Guess My Definition. Write *unbroken* on the board and underline the prefix *un-*. Point to the word *unbroken* and say to the class, "Guess my definition." Encourage students to think about the meaning of the prefix *un-* (not) and the meaning of the root word to determine the definition. Continue with the words *unhappy, uncommon, uncover, undecided, undo, uneven, unfair, unfold, untie,* and *unload*. If students have difficulty guessing the definitions, allow volunteers to use the words in sentences, act out scenes, or draw pictures to provide helpful clues.

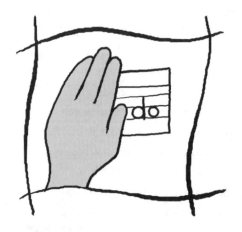

With or Without a Prefix?

Write the words *undo, uncover, uncle, unfit, under, until, unplug, unwrap, untrue,* and *understand* on index cards or sentence strips. Write *With a Prefix* at the top of a piece of chart paper and write *Without a Prefix* at the top of another piece. Explain that although *un-* is a common prefix, every word beginning with the letters *u* and *n* does not have a prefix at the beginning of it. If a root word remains after covering the letters *u* and *n*, then *un-* is a prefix. When *un-* is used as a prefix, it means *the opposite of* or *not*. Model how to use the "prefix test." To demonstrate, write the word *unlucky* on the board and cover the letters *u* and *n*. Ask, "Is *lucky* a word? Is *un-* a prefix in this word? If so, what do you think *unlucky* means?" Have students play the game With or Without a Prefix. Show one of the words and ask a volunteer to cover up *u* and *n*. Ask, "Is this a word with or without a prefix?" If the word has a prefix, ask students to define the word. Then, tape the word to the chart paper titled *With a Prefix*. If the *un* is not a prefix, tape the word to the chart paper titled *Without a Prefix*. Continue play with the rest of the words.

Building Words

Write the word *redo* on the board, underline the prefix *re-*, and share that *re-* is a prefix that means *again*. Point out that the root word of *redo* is *do*, so *redo* means to do something again. Write the word *refill* on the board and underline the prefix *re-*. Ask, "What do you think the word *refill* means?" Remind students that when they *refill* drinks at a restaurant, they fill their cups again. Give students more practice with the prefix *re-*. Distribute copies of the Building Words reproducible (page 62). Have each student cut out the prefixes at the bottom of the reproducible and glue them to the beginning of the root words. After students glue prefixes to root words, have students write the words' definitions. Remind students to think about the meaning of the prefix *re-* (again) and the meaning of each root word to determine the definition. Let students share their definitions.

What Sounds Right?

Explain that several prefixes mean *not*. Write the prefixes *un-*, *in-*, *im-*, *ir-*, *il-*, and *dis-* on the board. Share that all of these prefixes mean *not*. When deciding which prefix to use with a root word, have students ask themselves, "What sounds right?" Say two words, one with the correct prefix and the other with the incorrect prefix. Have students decide which word sounds right. Say, "*undo* and *disdo*. If you think *undo* uses the correct prefix for *not*, give a thumbs up." Count the thumbs and say, "If you think *disdo* has the correct prefix for *not*, give a thumbs up." Count the number of thumbs up and share that *undo* has the correct prefix. Write *undo* on the board. Continue the lesson with the words *ilimportant* and *unimportant*, *unwrap* and *diswrap*, *iltrue* and *untrue*, *irresponsible* and *unresponsible*, *unhonest* and *dishonest*, *disobey* and *unobey*, *impossible* and *ilpossible*, *displeased* and *unpleased*, *illike* and *dislike*, and *illegal* and *unlegal*. (Keep in mind that some students will think the incorrect form sounds right, so reteach accordingly.)

Building Words

Cut out the prefixes. Glue one
to the front of each root word. Define each word.

1. [ ] [fill]   definition: _____
   _____
   _____

2. [ ] [write]   definition: _____
   _____
   _____

3. [ ] [read]   definition: _____
   _____
   _____

4. [ ] [run]   definition: _____
   _____
   _____

5. [ ] [play]   definition: _____
   _____
   _____

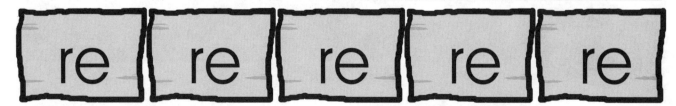

[re]   [re]   [re]   [re]   [re]

First-Rate Reading™: Vocabulary • CD-104020 • © Carson-Dellosa
Basics

More Than One

Write the word *pen* on the board and have a volunteer point to a pen in the classroom. Write *pens* on the board and underline the letter *s*. Tell students that the *s* at the end changes the definition to mean more than one. Have another student find more pens and hold them up under the word *pens*. Write the names of other classroom objects on the board, such as *pencil, chair, eraser, crayon, marker, ruler, backpack, book,* and *paper*. (Choose objects whose plural forms are made by adding *s*.) Label a piece of chart paper *One* and label another *More Than One*. Place the chart papers on the floor. Tell each student to choose one object from the list on the board, find that object, and place it on the chart paper labeled *One*. Then, have each student collect more than one of the object in a stack on the piece of chart paper labeled *More Than One*. Give each student two index cards to create labels—one label for the single object and the other for the multiple objects. Have students put the appropriate labels near the items. Then, let students look at the collections and read the labels.

Boxes of Foxes

Explain that the letters *e* and *s* at the end of a noun sometimes mean *more than one of that person, place,* or *thing*. Write the letters *s, x, z, ch,* and *sh* on the board. Explain that if a word ends in one of these letters and there is more than one of that thing, students should usually add *es*. For example, write the word *box* on the board and note that it means one box. Ask, "What is the last letter in the word *box*?" Explain that because the word ends with the letter *x*, students need to add *es* to mean more than one. Write the word *boxes* on the board and underline the *es*. Write the word *class* on the board and ask, "What is the last letter in the word *class*?" Share that since the last letter is *s*, students need to add *es* to mean more than one class. Write *classes* on the board. Give students additional practice adding *es* and pass out copies of the Boxes of Foxes reproducible (page 64). Instruct students to write the singular form of the words in the boxes that have one item, and the plural form of the words in the boxes that have more than one item. When students are finished, review the answers.

Name _____

Boxes of Foxes

Write the picture names on the
lines in the boxes. Add es to the singular names
to get the plural names.

First-Rate Reading™: Vocabulary • CD-104020 • © Carson-Dellosa
Basics

I Remember When

Explain that *-ed* is a suffix and write the word *play* on the board. Share that *play* means to play right now. Write the word *played* on the board and underline the letters *e* and *d*. Tell the class that the suffix *-ed* means something has already happened. Share a few sample sentences: "I played with my friend yesterday. We already played that game." Give each student an I Remember When reproducible (page 66) and write the root words *talk, play, shout, sprint, bark, wait, ask, rain, snow, work, open, list, walk, visit,* and *paint* on the board. Share that some people put photos of special events in scrapbooks and write about them. Let each student choose a word from the list and use the word in a sentence about a life experience. Have students write and illustrate their sentences in the boxes on the reproducibles. Have each student cut apart the boxes and glue them to a piece of black construction paper. Allow students to use chalk, white paint, or metallic markers to label their pages. Collect the

pages, add a front and back cover, and write the title *We Remember When* on the front. Read one page each day beginning with, "(Student's name) remembers when . . ." Allow students to point out the verbs that use *-ed* when you finish reading. Let the featured student explain his sentences to the class.

Walking Stick

Bring a real walking stick (or a cane) to class or create one from a large stick or piece of tagboard. On the handle, tie a piece of paper with *-ing* written on it. Remind students that adding a suffix to a root word changes the meaning of the word. Write the word *walk* on the board and say, "I walk to school." Explain that in this sentence, *walk* means this person walks to school. Write the word *walking* on the board and explain that *-ing* is a suffix. Say, "I am walking to the playground. This sentence means I am walking right now." Work with students to add the suffix *-ing* to other verbs. Write the words *talk, play, shout, bark, wait, ask, work,* and *paint* on the board. Ask for a volunteer to remove the *-ing* sign from the walking stick and place it at the end of a word. Have the class read the word and challenge students to think of a sentence using the word. Then, have a volunteer place the *-ing* sign at the end of another word. Repeat the process with the rest of the root words. Finally, give each student a craft stick to represent a walking stick. Read a picture book with several *-ing* words in it. As you read aloud, have students pretend to use their walking sticks when they hear *-ing* words.

Name _____

I Remember When

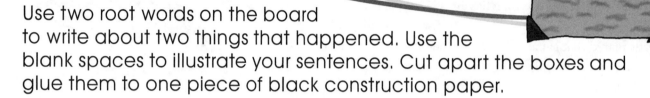

Use two root words on the board to write about two things that happened. Use the blank spaces to illustrate your sentences. Cut apart the boxes and glue them to one piece of black construction paper.

Context Clues: Introduction

Most of these activities need reading selections to go with them. When choosing a text, remember that the meanings of the unfamiliar words should be understandable from the context. The activities in this section help students use context clues, determine the importance of surrounding words, and consider homophones carefully. Remind students to use reference aids when context clues do not provide enough information to understand new words.

Flibbidy Fun

Explain that readers can figure out the meanings of unknown words by looking at the surrounding words. Say, "I love sprinkling *flibbidy* on my ice cream. It is so colorful!" Ask students to use the clues in the sentences to define the nonsense word *flibbidy*. Ask students for suggestions and continue using *flibbidy* in the sentences listed below. Each time, ask students to use clues to define the nonsense word.

Sentences:

1. My brother drives a *flibbidy*. It is so fast!
2. It was cold outside, so I wore my *flibbidy*. It kept my head nice and warm.
3. I grew the biggest *flibbidy* in my garden. I picked it and put it in a vase.
4. Yesterday, I went to a *flibbidy* game. Our team made 30 baskets!
5. Last vacation, I rode the *flibbidy* at the amusement park. It went so high and then came down to make a fast loop.

Vocabulary Quiz

Choose 10 vocabulary words that are difficult and new for students. For each word, prepare one sentence with context clues. Give each student a piece of paper and a pencil. Read a vocabulary word without its surrounding sentence and ask students to write definitions for the word. Because these words are isolated and new to students, this part of the activity should be a challenge. Continue with the remaining words. After students have defined the vocabulary words, have them turn over their papers. Read each vocabulary word in its sentence. Have students write definitions now using the context clues. Reveal the actual definitions, then ask, "Was it more helpful to have a sentence with each word? Did you have an easier time defining the words when they were in sentences?" Tell the class that the same is true in reading. Often, the sentences containing the words and the surrounding sentences help readers understand the meanings of new words.

Extra Eyes

Remind students that all readers encounter new words, and learning these words helps readers better understand what they are reading. One strategy for figuring out the meanings of these words is to look for clues in the sentences. Explain that students will make extra pairs of eyes to help them look for clues. Give each student a craft stick, a pair of wiggly eyes, and glue. Have each student glue two wiggly eyes onto the end of the craft stick and allow them to dry. Select five vocabulary words from a reading lesson. Choose words that are unfamiliar to students and that can be understood from context clues. On the board, write sentences that contain the words and context clues. Read one sentence and stop reading. Have students use their "extra eyes" (and their own eyes) to reread the sentence. Encourage a few students to come to the board and move their "extra eyes" under each word to help them track print (focus on the words). Ask, "Do you see any clues that help us figure out the word's meaning?" If students do not find any clues, share some context clues and help students understand the meaning of the word. Continue reading and help students look for clues for the remaining words. Close the lesson by saying, "When you come to a word in your reading that you don't recognize, look for clues in the surrounding sentences." Encourage students to use their "extra eyes" to track print in other reading lessons.

Put It in Context

Write each of the following sets of sentences on a separate piece of chart paper: 1. *He saw a <u>gnu</u> in the zoo. It looked like a buffalo with very large horns.* 2. *A wild <u>boar</u> ran across the desert. Its three piglets ran after it.* 3. *He noticed a <u>herd</u> of deer. Some of them had antlers and some did not.* 4. *The praying mantis has a <u>flexible</u> neck. It can turn its head in many directions to look for its food.* 5. *I saw a <u>slug</u> in our garden. It looked like a snail without a shell.* Post the papers around the classroom. Remind students that sometimes readers can figure out the meanings of words by looking for clues in surrounding sentences. For example, ask, "Who can tell me what a *gibbon* is?" If no one answers, write the following sentences  on the board: *The gibbon lives in Asia. Like other apes, it has no tail.* Read the first sentence and share that there is a clue in that sentence—a *gibbon* is a living thing found in Asia. Read the second sentence and note the clues—a gibbon has no tail and is an ape. Ask, "Now, what do you think a gibbon is?" Assign students to five small groups and position each group near one of the pieces of chart paper. Have group members read their sentences and look for clues that tell the meanings of the underlined words. When each group comes to a consensus, have a volunteer write the definition below their sentence. Then, have volunteers from each group read their sentences and definitions. Share the correct definitions with the class.

Translation Time

Ask, "How many of you can speak French?" Explain that many words in the English language actually came from French words. But just like other unknown words, students can figure out these words' meanings by looking at the surrounding words. Share that helpful context clues can make the meanings of these words "magically" appear. Voilà! Give each student a copy of the Translation Time reproducible (page 70). Share that the underlined words have French origins. Have students read the sentences, or read them aloud to students. Help students write definitions of the words under each of the sentences. Have students use dictionaries to compare their definitions to the correct ones. After students finish, review the answers. Consider doing a similar activity with words with Spanish origins, such as *armadillo, cinch, tornado, enchilada, poncho*, etc.

Looking for Clues

Choose three vocabulary words from a current reading lesson that are unfamiliar to students but have context clues in surrounding sentences. Explain that it is important to learn the meanings of those words so that they can comprehend what they are reading. Share that detectives look for clues to solve mysteries. Tell students that they are going to be word detectives. Write the vocabulary words on the board and distribute the Looking for Clues reproducible (page 71). Have each student copy the three words onto her reproducible. Begin the reading lesson. After reading one of the words, stop reading. Work with students to find clues in surrounding sentences and have students write clues under the word. Then, help students write the meaning of the word in their own words. Repeat the process with the remaining vocabulary words. At the end of the lesson, encourage students to look for clues when they encounter new words.

Translation Time

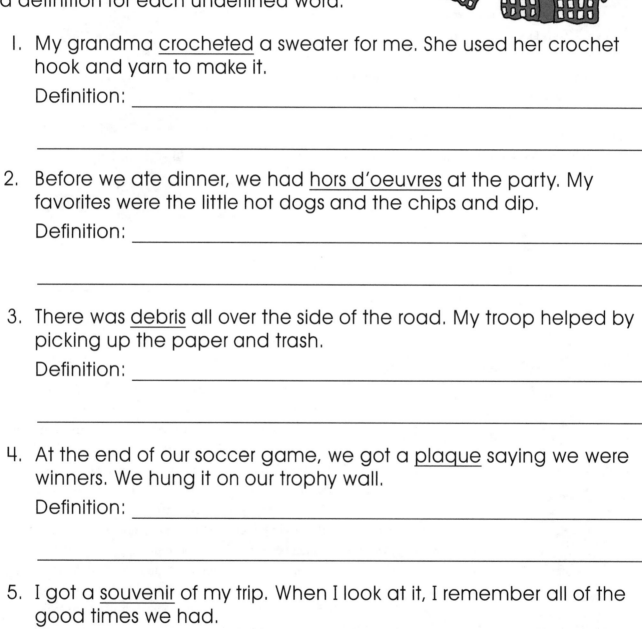

Use the context clues to write
a definition for each underlined word.

1. My grandma <u>crocheted</u> a sweater for me. She used her crochet
   hook and yarn to make it.
   Definition: _____

   _____

2. Before we ate dinner, we had <u>hors d'oeuvres</u> at the party. My
   favorites were the little hot dogs and the chips and dip.
   Definition: _____

   _____

3. There was <u>debris</u> all over the side of the road. My troop helped by
   picking up the paper and trash.
   Definition: _____

   _____

4. At the end of our soccer game, we got a <u>plaque</u> saying we were
   winners. We hung it on our trophy wall.
   Definition: _____

   _____

5. I got a <u>souvenir</u> of my trip. When I look at it, I remember all of the
   good times we had.
   Definition: _____

   _____

First-Rate Reading™: Vocabulary • CD-104020 • © Carson-Dellosa
Basics

Looking for Clues

Write each vocabulary word,
its context clues, and its meaning next to a magnifying glass.

1. Vocabulary Word: _____

   Context Clues: _____

   _____

   _____

   Meaning: _____

   _____

2. Vocabulary Word: _____

   Context Clues: _____

   _____

   _____

   Meaning: _____

   _____

3. Vocabulary Word: _____

   Context Clues: _____

   _____

   _____

   Meaning: _____

   _____

Helpful or Not Helpful?

Write each sentence or sentences below on a sentence strip. Explain that sometimes the strategy of looking at context clues will not help students understand new words. Hold up and read the first sentence strip. Ask, "Do the clues in these sentences help us understand the underlined word?" If the sentences are helpful, keep the sentence strip; if the sentences are not helpful, put it aside. Continue with the rest of the sentences. After students have sorted the sentences, return to the stack of helpful ones. Work with students to use the clues to define the underlined words. At the end of the lesson, remind students to consider whether surrounding words and sentences are helpful. When there are no helpful context clues, recommend that students use reference tools to define new words in text. (Sentences 2, 4, 8, and 10 do not have helpful clues.)

1. We keep our kitchen supplies and food in the <u>pantry</u>.
2. She is very <u>patient</u>.
3. I wrote my letter on <u>stationery</u>. The paper had pretty flowers on it.
4. My teacher is my <u>inspiration</u>.
5. He <u>gargled</u> with salt and water to get rid of his sore throat.
6. She gave me a <u>compliment</u>. She said that I looked very nice today.
7. My grandpa was an <u>immigrant</u>. He came all the way from Ireland to live in this country.
8. He looked <u>confident</u>.
9. The <u>customers</u> came into the store and bought some shoes.
10. She did not seem <u>concerned</u>.

It's in the Bag

Write the following sentences on a paper bag: *After Jim didn't make the basketball team, he persevered. He practiced every day, no matter what, so that he could try again next year.* Have students use the strategy of looking for clues in surrounding sentences in a classroom contest. (Hold this contest just once, every day, or every week, depending on students' needs and interests). Show students the sentences on the paper bag and give each student one index card. Have students write their names on the cards. Read the sentences on the first bag to the class and say, "What do you think *persevered* means? Write the definition on your index cards." Have students place their index cards in the paper bag. Find all of the cards that have the correct definition, share the correct definition, and announce the winners. Complete the same activity with other vocabulary words. When everyone in class wins, let students bring bag lunches and eat outside or in the classroom on blankets.

Three Chances

Select at least 10 new vocabulary words from a lesson plan. For each vocabulary word, write three sentences that contain context clues, such as, *We checked the thermometer to see if today was colder than yesterday. The weather person uses a thermometer to check the day's high temperature. My mom put a thermometer in my mouth to see if I had a fever.* To play Three Chances, assign students to five teams. Read a vocabulary word in a sentence. Team A should work together to define the word. If they give the correct definition after the first sentence, give them three points. If they do not give the correct definition, read a second sentence containing the word. The team members should talk to each other and guess again. If they are correct, give them two points. If they are incorrect, read the third sentence and let them present their definition. If Team A is correct on the third try, give them one point. If they are incorrect, give Teams B through E one chance each to guess the definition. If another team gets the correct answer, they get one point. Continue until all words have been correctly defined, starting with a different team each time. The team with the most points at the end of the game wins. If there is a tie, reward the winning teams.

Message in a Bottle

Remind students that sometimes there are clues for new words in surrounding sentences. Give each student a copy of the Message in a Bottle reproducible (page 74). Explain that students will write messages to each other. Tell each student to cut out his paper bottle, choose a hard word from the dictionary, and then read the definition. (Give students guidance in choosing appropriate words, or assign a word to each student.) Have each student write the definition of her word on one side of the bottle and write one or two sentences using the vocabulary word on the other side. Encourage students to put enough clues in the sentences so that a reader can define the words without looking at the definitions. When students are finished, have each student place her bottle in the "sea" (a table covered with a blue cloth). Then, let each student choose a bottle that is not her own, read the sentence, try to figure out the mystery word, and then check her prediction against the definition on the back of the bottle to see if her guess was correct.

Name _____

Message in a Bottle

Cut out the bottle. Choose a hard word. Write its definition on the back. Write sentences using the word and context clues on the front.

First-Rate Reading™: Vocabulary • CD-104020 • © Carson-Dellosa
Basics

Homophone Help

Explain that sometimes two words sound the same but have very different meanings. Write the words *see* and *sea* on the board and read both words. Note that the words sound exactly the same, but one word means to look at, and the other word means a large body of water. Point out that the words are spelled differently, but sometimes it is difficult to remember which spelling and meaning go together. Explain that one way to remember the meanings is to look for clues in the surrounding words and sentences. Give each student a copy of the Homophone Help reproducible (page 76). Explain that the sentences include words that sound the same. Instruct students to use the clues in the sentences to figure out the meanings of the words. Read the first two sentences to the class, have

students use the clues in the sentences to define the words *eight* and *ate*, and have students write their definitions below the sentences. Continue with the rest of the sentences. At the end of the lesson, share the answers with the class. Remind students to use context clues to understand homophones.

Mystery Meanings

Choose a vocabulary word from a reading, science, or social studies unit, character education program, etc. On sentence strips, write five sentences with context clues for the word. Fold the sentence strips in half and write Clue 1, Clue 2, etc., on the backs. Each day, hide a clue in an obvious location in the classroom—hang it from the ceiling, place the clue in the arms of a stuffed animal, etc. Share that there is a classroom mystery for students to solve, and each day there will be a new clue to help them define a vocabulary word. Have students look for and find the first clue, open it, and read the sentence. Ask students to guess the definition, but do not confirm or correct the definition until students have opened all five clues. On the last day, review the clues and work with the class to define the word. Consider having a classroom mystery each week to increase students' vocabularies and give them practice using context clues.

Homophone Help

Read each sentence. Define each underlined word.

1. I am <u>eight</u> years old.

   Definition: _____

2. He <u>ate</u> pizza for dinner.

   Definition: _____

3. It was a sunny day. The sky was bright <u>blue</u>.

   Definition: _____

4. When I <u>blew</u> on the pinwheel, it turned really fast.

   Definition: _____

5. The <u>bear</u> and her cub were walking through the woods.

   Definition: _____

6. I couldn't find anything to eat. The refrigerator was <u>bare</u>.

   Definition: _____

7. She picked a <u>flower</u> from the garden and put it in a vase.

   Definition: _____

8. The cook used <u>flour</u> to make the cake.

   Definition: _____

9. I like chocolate ice cream best, <u>too</u>.

   Definition: _____

10. We are going to the beach tomorrow at <u>two</u> o'clock.

    Definition: _____

First-Rate Reading™: Vocabulary • CD-104020 • © Carson-Dellosa
Basics

Fortune Cookie Fun

Ask, "Has anyone ever had a fortune cookie?" Explain that a fortune cookie is a small cookie with a message inside it. Consider providing a box of real, edible examples. (Get families' permission and inquire about food allergies and religious and other food preferences.) Give each student a copy of the Fortune Cookie Fun reproducible (page 78). Have students open dictionaries and choose difficult words. Challenge each student to write a sentence containing the word and context clues. Give an example using the word *dinosaur.* Write *Ted's favorite animal is the dinosaur, because he loves prehistoric creatures.* Ask, "Which words are clues to the meaning of the word *dinosaur?*" (The sentence states that a dinosaur was an animal and that it lived long ago.) Have students write their sentences on the strips on the reproducibles and underline the words. Have each student cut out the strip and circle, put the sentence in the middle of the circle, dot glue around the circle's edges, and fold the top over the bottom like a sandwich. Have students press the edges together and let the "fortune cookies" dry. Give each student a classmate's fortune cookie and have him carefully pull out the strip. Then, have students read the sentences, look for clues, and write definitions for the underlined words on the backs of the strips. Have students check their definitions by looking up the words in dictionaries.

Vocabulary Octopus

Announce that students will play Vocabulary Octopus. Choose a vocabulary word that will be new and difficult for students. Write a sentence containing the vocabulary word and context clues on the board, but leave out the vocabulary word. Instead, write a small line for each letter in the vocabulary word. Refer to the illustration (left). Draw the head of an octopus to the side of the sentence. Have students look for clues in the sentence and guess the letters that are in the word. If students guess correctly, write the letters in the matching blanks. If students guess incorrectly, add one leg to the octopus and write the incorrect letter near that leg. Continue having students look at the clues and guess the letters. If students guess the word before the octopus has eight legs, the class wins.

Name _____

Fortune Cookie Fun

Write a sentence that uses a
difficult word on the strip. Write your name below
the sentence. Cut out the strip and the circle. Place the strip in the
center of the circle. Add dots of glue on the dots and fold the circle in
half. Then, press the edges together and let it dry.

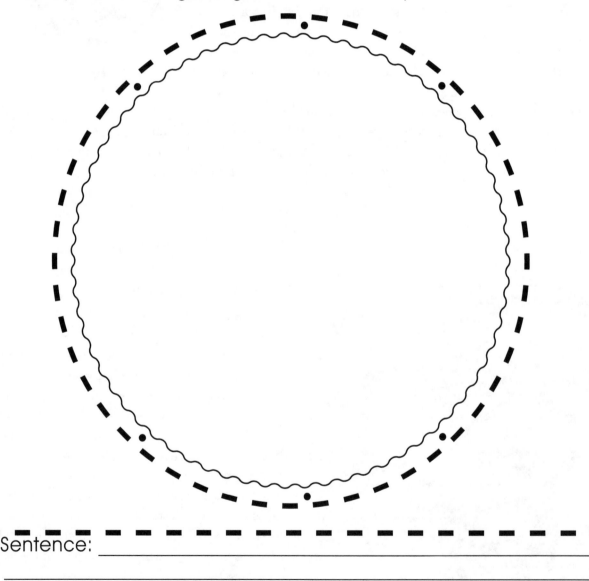

Sentence: _____
_____
by _____

First-Rate Reading™: Vocabulary • CD-104020 • © Carson-Dellosa
Basics

Weather Words

Choose four important and new vocabulary words from a nonfiction text about weather. Cover up the four words in the actual text with removable white tape. Write each word on a piece of sentence strip. Show the book's cover to the class and have students predict what the book will be about. Begin reading the selected text. Students should notice a blank space in the text. Show them the first word and ask which word on the sentence strip makes the most sense based on the context clues (the surrounding words and sentences). After students have decided on a word, reread the sentence with their choice in the blank. If needed, guide students toward the appropriate word and continue reading. Repeat the process with the three other vocabulary words. To extend the activity, write the words on the board. Gather props that pertain to the vocabulary words and place them in a paper bag. (For example, place a resealable plastic bag of dry, brown grass or sand in the paper bag for the vocabulary word *drought*.) Have students pass the paper bag while listening to music. When the music stops, the student holding the bag should close his eyes, pull something out of the bag, and identify the corresponding weather word.

I have gone to the <u>grocery store</u> to renew my book. Be back soon.

Mixed-Up Message

If students are not familiar with the concept of a morning message, share that some teachers write messages, or short letters, to their classes to start each school day. Distribute a Mixed-Up Message reproducible (page 80) to each student. Have each student read the message and think about the context clues to replace the underlined words with words that make sense. After everyone is finished, have volunteers share how they filled in the blanks. Ask students to explain how they knew which words made sense. For an extra challenge, have students write their own mixed-up messages on the backs of the reproducibles. Assign partners to students, have them switch messages, and replace the underlined words. Listen to students read the messages to make sure their responses make sense within the context of the sentences. Answer key: 1. Hello; 2. library; 3. rainy; 4. day 5. Sincerely; 6. outside

Mixed-Up Message

Read the morning message below. Replace the underlined words with words that make sense. Write the new words in the blanks below.

Goodbye class,

   Today is Monday. We will check out books at the grocery store and then have art. We will eat outside if it is not wet and salty. We have a new student. Her name is Felicia. Please help her feel welcome. Today will be a great evening!

                    Happily,
                    Ms. Seltzer

P.S. If you clean up calmly and quickly today, we will go inside and play kickball for an extra 10 minutes.

---

1. Goodbye _____   2. grocery store _____

3. salty _____   4. evening _____

5. Happily _____   6. inside _____

First-Rate Reading™: Vocabulary • CD-104020 • © Carson-Dellosa
Basics